SHORT WALK

Northamptonshire Pubs

Charles Whynne-Hammond

COUNTRYSIDE BOOKS
NEWBURY, BERKSHIRE

COUNTRYSIDE BOOKS
3 Catherine Road
Newbury, Berkshire

ISBN 1 85306 354 1

Cover illustration by Colin Doggett
Photographs and maps by Glenys Jones

Produced through MRM Associates Ltd., Reading
Typeset by Paragon Typesetters, Clwyd
Printed by Woolnough Bookbinding Ltd., Irthlingborough

Contents

Publisher's Note

We hope that you obtain considerable enjoyment from this book; great care has been taken in its preparation. However, changes of landlord and actual closures are sadly not uncommon. Likewise, although at the time of publication all routes followed public rights of way or permitted paths, diversion orders can be made and permissions withdrawn.

We cannot of course be held responsible for such diversion orders and any resultant inaccuracies in the text which result from these or any other changes to the routes nor any damage which might result from walkers trespassing on private property. We are anxious that all details covering the walks and the pubs are kept up to date and would therefore welcome information from readers which would be relevant to future editions.

Area map showing locations of the walks.

Introduction

Northamptonshire has some of the loveliest countryside in middle England. There are woods, hills and valleys; broad meadow lands and rolling uplands; wildlife nature reserves and landscaped parklands. There are also numerous canals and reservoirs; old railway lines, some of which have been transformed into footpaths; ancient trackways along which foot traffic has continued for centuries; and long distance footpaths designated in more recent years for the enjoyment of walkers. The villages of Northamptonshire are quiet and unspoilt; the farmlands bear the imprint of past agricultural practices, from the ridge-and-furrow of feudal strip cultivation to the quickthorn-fringed fields of the 18th century enclosure movement. In short, this county of ours has a wide and varied landscape.

The walks in this book reflect this variety, offering a range of routes across different kinds of terrain. Many of the ones described include shorter or longer options. These will allow readers to design walks to suit themselves, or else to undertake more than one walk from each starting point. In addition there are suggestions, in the text, for routes (or parts of routes) that can be done by those who are pushing prams or wheelchairs. There is no reason why those people with young children, or with disabled friends and relatives, should not be able to enjoy the countryside as well as everybody else.

The Ordnance Survey maps referred to in the book are from the 1:50,000 Landranger series. These are invaluable to walkers as they show the features of the landscape, and public rights of way, on a scale suitable for the average length walks. All the rights of way should be walkable. Readers who find any difficulty with a public footpath should telephone the local authority, which is responsible for maintaining such routes.

Generally pubs still keep normal opening times – 11 am or 11.30 am to 2.30 pm lunchtimes, 6.30 pm or 7 pm to 11 pm evenings. These hours may be extended slightly on Saturdays and reduced slightly on Sundays. Those wishing to eat should aim for the reasonable 'sitting' times: 12 noon to 1.30 pm and 7 pm to 10 pm. Variations in 'normal' pub times are given in the text. Most of the pubs listed have car parks and landlords allow customers to leave their vehicles on the premises while going for a short walk. However, it would be polite to inform those landlords first before doing so.

All the pubs in this book welcome families with children, both inside and out. Most have gardens where children can play, together with 'family rooms', or else rooms specifically used by families. All the establishments are friendly, helpful and comfortable. Today, the quality and variety of food on offer in pubs is exceptional and all the places listed have menus that should satisfy even the most discerning of tastes. Real ales are now widely available. The food and drink items in the pub profiles are, of course, given only as examples of the refreshments offered. They do not aim to give comprehensive lists. Any special dietary requirements should be addressed to the landlords, who are usually only too happy to co-operate.

I should like to thank all those pub proprietors who supplied me with valuable information regarding their establishments. I am also indebted to Glenys Jones for drawing the maps, and to Gwen Cassell who helped with the final draft.

Charles Whynne-Hammond
Spring 1995

① Helmdon
The Bell Inn

Said to date back to the 17th century this building used to be a farmhouse. And although it has been a pub for over 100 years there is still much of the farmhouse atmosphere about it. Inside there are low beams, flagstone floors and simple country-style furniture.

The public bar and lounge, although separate, are so interconnected that they almost act as one room. At one end there is a pool room, where further seating is provided – and it is here where families tend to gather. Children are indeed welcome and facilities for them are provided in the garden. Open fires burn during the colder times of the year; these adding to the cosy, friendly ambience.

Various real ales are offered including Theakston and Marston's Pedigree. The food served is mainly of the bar snack variety – with rolls, sandwiches, ploughman's lunches and salads. The portions are large and well presented, and the quality is excellent.

Telephone: 01295 768155.

How to get there: Helmdon stands just 4 miles north of Brackley and 8 miles south-west of Towcester. It is close to the border with Buckinghamshire – Buckingham itself is only 10 miles away south-eastwards. The village lies just off the B4525 road. The Bell Inn is in Church Street, at the southern end of Helmdon.

Parking: There is a pub car park. Vehicles can also be left, within reason, anywhere in the village, for the streets are not busy.

Length of the walk: 3 miles (longer or shorter options). OS Landranger map 152 Northampton and Milton Keynes (inn GR 588436).

Helmdon stands in hilly countryside and is surrounded by well-trodden, well signposted footpaths. It is, therefore, an excellent centre from which to explore south-west Northamptonshire. Those wishing to do a longer circular route than the one described here may like to walk eastwards to Astwell House and back. Astwell is the site of a medieval castle. The walk route featured below circles Helmdon using clear footpaths that cross farmland. The length of the village is about one mile, and a walk down the High Street is included. To the west of Helmdon is the line of a disused railway and this is seen during the second part of the route.

The Walk
From the Bell Inn walk up Church Street, in a southerly direction – that is, away from the main part of Helmdon village. There is a footpath along here, off to the left, and you could take this, thus shortening the circuit. But the footpath that leads from the church offers better views so that is the one recommended in this description.

The church, which dates from the 13th century, stands at the top of Church Street, on the very edge of the village. It occupies an ancient, hilltop position and boasts, in its churchyard, a yew tree said to be 2,000 years old.

The footpath required leads from the back of the churchyard, reached by walking past the tombstones keeping the church on your right-hand side. Follow the stone wall as it rounds a corner, to the left, and you will see a kissing gate in front. The path leads beyond this, along by a wooden fence. This is a pleasant walk, with open fields to the right, the village to the left and, ahead on the skyline, the northern end of Helmdon, for which you are aiming. In due course you go through another kissing gate and continue in the same direction, ignoring two stiles and footpaths on the right and another path on the left. Those intending to walk to Astwell should follow the second footpath on the right.

Through two more kissing gates, you go half right to cross a field diagonally where another kissing gate takes you to a path that runs along a field edge, with the hedgerow on your right. There is a stile in this hedgerow, halfway, and this leads to another route to Astwell, to be followed by those interested. Those not interested, will reach a

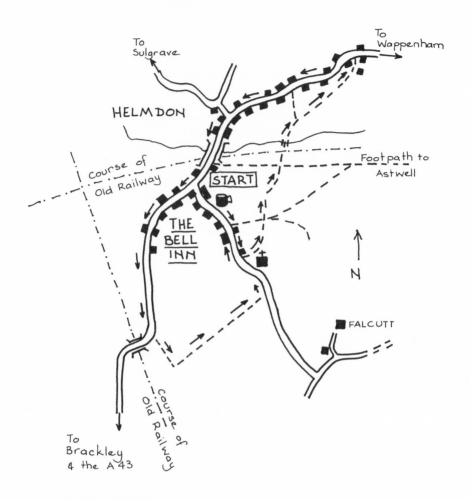

To Sulgrave

To Wappenham

HELMDON

Course of Old Railway

START

Footpath to Astwell

THE BELL INN

N

FALCUTT

Course of Old Railway

To Brackley & the A43

wide, wooden footbridge across a stream. On the far side bear half-right, along a grassy path that runs diagonally up to the houses on the skyline. There, close to the left corner of the stone house, a stile takes you to a tarmac lane. This (called Fieldway) leads to the village street, where you turn left, to walk down the entire length of Helmdon.

This is an attractive village, with a pleasing mixture of architecture: medieval, Victorian and modern, stone and brick. The stone buildings recall the fact that Helmdon was once famous for its limestone quarries. The stone from these was used for large parts of Brackley and Towcester. During the 19th century Helmdon also grew as a railway village, two lines crossing here, one running east-west from

10

Helmdon Village.

Northampton to Oxford, the other running north-south from Birmingham to Brackley.

Walking downhill along the main street keep to the left at the junction where stands the War Memorial. At the bottom is a fork. To the left is Church Street, along which stands the Bell Inn. Those wishing to shorten the walk can turn here. Others should keep right, to follow the lane round past the village school and, opposite, a building that was once another pub. Further up, beyond the edge of the village, this lane bends right and left as it crosses the bridge over the old railway line.

The footpath back begins on the left, just before this bridge. A stile leads you to a track that runs along the top of the railway cutting. In due course turn left over another stile. The path now crosses two fields in a straight line ending along a stretch of track that runs between hedges some 20 feet apart. At the end of this is the road. Turn left to walk past the church, back down to the Bell Inn.

Places of interest nearby

Sulgrave Manor, ancestral home of the Washington family, is just 2 miles away north-westwards. South-east of Helmdon, in Buckinghamshire, are the *Stowe Landscaped Gardens*. These surround the famous public school and are managed by the National Trust.

2 Byfield
The Cross Tree

This was once called the New Inn. The present name comes from the tree that was planted next to the stump of an old market cross, still to be seen near the War Memorial, a little way north of the village green. In medieval times this cross was also used as a barter cross, where deals were struck.

This Banks's house, owned by Wolverhampton and Dudley Breweries, is open during normal pub times. It is very much a village local, with an interior thankfully devoid of 'olde worlde' kitsch. The public bar, to the left as you enter, has an area given over to games, with a pool table, dartboard and skittles table. The lounge bar, to the right, is rather more plush with soft bench seats, carpet and a piano. Throughout there are beams, trophies and pictures decorating the walls, and a general atmosphere of friendliness. Families are welcome and there are children's playthings in the garden.

Real ales served include Banks's and Marston's Pedigree, and the draught cider is Strongbow. Apart from the usual house wines there is also a selection of English fruit wines, like elderberry and cherry. The blackboard in the public bar lists a wide range of food and this should satisfy everyone. Bar snacks include rolls, sandwiches (normal

and toasted), ploughman's; main meals include steaks, grills, scampi, chilli and so on; vegetarian dishes include lasagne and broccoli and mushroom mornay. Portions are generous and, therefore, good value.
Telephone: 01327 60391.

How to get there: Byfield stands on the A361 Banbury road, 8 miles south-west of Daventry. It is close to the Warwickshire border, amongst the hills that are a continuation of the Cotswolds. Brackley is some 12 miles distant, to the south-east. The Cross Tree will be found facing the A361 at the southern end of the village.

Parking: There is a pub car park. Vehicles can also be left along the side streets of Byfield but, preferably, not along the A361 which can be busy.

Length of the walk: 5 miles (or shorter option). OS Landranger map 151 Stratford-upon-Avon (inn GR 516531).

There are many pleasant walks around Byfield, for this is a lovely part of Northamptonshire. One route circumnavigates Boddington reservoir, which lies just a mile west of the village. Another leads east to Hinton and returns from West Farndon. The walk here described is to the village of Aston le Walls and back. The outward journey is by a bridleway. The return journey is by footpaths across farmland. One short section, on the return route, runs alongside Boddington reservoir, popular with anglers and yachtsmen alike. The route is well marked throughout with signposts and arrow discs. There are some stiles to climb but there are no steep slopes and the walking conditions are relatively easy.

The Walk
The route begins along New Terrace, which runs behind the Cross Tree. At the end of this, turn left along Banbury Lane and then, almost immediately, right along Bell Lane. This kinks right then left, as it passes a house that was once a pub called The Bell, and ends at a T-junction, which marks the western end of Byfield. The bridleway opposite is the way ahead, leading to Aston le Walls.

The bridleway to Aston le Walls, at first, is a wide gravel lane, for it once led to the Byfield railway sidings. At that point it kinks, as it goes over the bridge that crosses the non-existent line, and becomes less clear, continuing as a grassy track. You follow it between fields to an old barn, where a slight left bend takes you into the field above (at the bottom of the slope that leads up to Golden Hill). Now continue in the same direction as before keeping the hedge to your right. The views on the right are beginning to open out towards Warwickshire. On a clear day the prospect is beautiful.

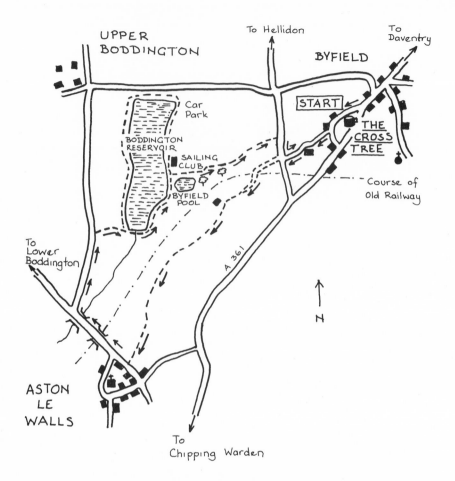

The way to Aston is fairly straightforward, and arrow discs mark the way at each gate. From the field corner cross diagonally over the brow of a small hill and then aim slightly left, alongside a hedge, to follow a track that leads on between hedgerows. Thereafter you follow the edges of two fields to another length of trackway and then a further length of field edge to the top corner where two farm gates present themselves. Go through the one on the right and continue across the valley ahead. Keeping the hedge to your left along this next stretch you will eventually come to the road at Aston le Walls.

Those not wishing to look round Aston should turn right along the road, which is a country lane and not very busy. The village is an attractive place, with a church dating back to Norman times and an 18th century Hall.

14

Norman church at Aston le Walls.

The road walk is a little over a mile, but very pleasant with views both sides. Down in the valley you cross the stream and, immediately, turn right along a smaller lane signposted to Upper Boddington and Priors Hardwick. This climbs steeply uphill. A few hundred yards beyond an old farm building, which you pass on your right, a footpath runs across the road. Follow the way that goes off to the right. Through the gate, follow the field edge eastwards, keeping the hedgerow to your left. Soon you will see Boddington reservoir ahead. Now cut across the field aiming for the right-hand end of the lake. There, in the corner, a gate leads through to the waterside.

Continue along the top of the dam and turn sharply left to follow the water's edge on the far side. This is a pleasant little path, running under the trees and through the undergrowth. In due course you pass, on the right, the small area of water set aside as a nature reserve and called Byfield Pool. A footbridge carries you across the outlet to this area and on to the sailing club car park. The route back to Byfield begins from this car parking area. As you emerge from the trees, and before you reach the club house, turn sharp right to reach a stile, half-hidden in the undergrowth. A further stile beyond leads through to a field where you turn right to follow the edge of the woodland. In the far corner another stile, and a plank bridge lead through to the next field where, after about 100 yards you turn right through a thicket. Here a stile and another plank bridge take you out to an open field.

The rest of the way is easy. Cross diagonally up over this field, follow the edge of the next field (hedge on right) and then, beyond further stiles, aim diagonally towards the spire of Byfield church. Along the edge of the last field you eventually come to the road. Turn right to reach the beginning of the bridleway that you followed at the beginning of the walk. From here you can retrace your steps to the Cross Tree.

Places of interest nearby

Canons Ashby House, (4 miles south-east of Byfield), is a 16th century manor house owned by the National Trust and once inhabited by the Dryden family. *Farnborough Hall* is 6 miles south-westwards and is a fine classical building, also owned by the National Trust. North of there is a country park near *Fenny Compton* where there are panoramic views from the Burton Hills.

③ Charwelton
The Fox and Hounds

The decor here is traditional but not 'olde worlde'. The beams are not original nor the furniture rustic. All is light and airy, with carpets on the floors and cushioned seats. In short, the Fox and Hounds has been renovated.

But this should not put off those who enjoy the old-fashioned type of village pub. For this is a very lively, friendly place that welcomes everyone, from locals to tourists, from walkers to families. Real ales are served (including Worthington and Bass), draught cider is on tap and wines are available from a chill-dispenser. And the food on offer is superb. Apart from the usual pub items, listed in the menu on the bar counter, there are numerous daily specials listed on the blackboard. These might include all manner of dishes – steaks, pies, quiches, seafood platters and so on. But it is the large choice of vegetarian meals that makes this pub fare unusual. Half-a-dozen or so offerings are listed including pasta, chilli and vegetable bakes.

To the left as you enter, is a large open-plan bar room, with sections for darts and quiet drinking. To the right, and stretching back, is a large lounge and dining area, where eaters and families tend to sit. Beyond the bar is the patio garden, at the rear of the building.

This freehouse keeps normal pub opening times.
Telephone: 01327 62358.

How to get there: Charwelton stands on the A361 Banbury road only
5 miles south-west of Daventry. Woodford Halse is 2 miles south, the
Warwickshire border 2 miles west. The Fox and Hounds will be found
on the left-hand side of the main road, as you drive from Daventry.

Parking: There is a car park at the rear of the pub and a few cars can
be parked at the roadside in front. But elsewhere along the A361
parking is not encouraged, owing to the volume of traffic. Vehicles
may be left in the quiet end of Charwelton, along the road to Church
Charwelton.

Length of the walk: 5 miles (or shorter option). OS Landranger map 152
Northampton and Milton Keynes (inn GR 535560).

*This is a hilly part of Northamptonshire: Arbury Hill and Badby Down are a short
distance north of Charwelton, Hinton Hill is a little to the south. The countryside
hereabouts is beautiful, and the views are uninterrupted. All the footpaths used are
clearly signposted. However, there are some stiles to climb and fenced hedges to
negotiate.*

*The route incorporates two historic sites: Church Charwelton (site of a medieval
village) and the Fawsley Estate (one-time home of the Knightley family). Fawsley
Park, with its lakes and isolated church, is a well-known picnic spot.*

The Walk
The first leg of the circular walk involves a pleasant stroll down a
country lane to Church Charwelton. It is a 'no through road' and
therefore very quiet. It is also a 'gated road', and therefore very pretty.

By turning left down the main road from the Fox and Hounds, and
then left again up a side lane, you reach the old and attractive end of
Charwelton, where stone cottages and neatly-kept gardens cluster
around a village hall. Follow the sign pointing the way to the church,
which is left at the fork. This lane leads down beside a little row of
houses and out into the countryside, bearing left to cross a stream, and
right to lead over the line of a disused railway. This was the track that
led from Rugby to Brackley via Woodford Halse. Today it is a grassy
thoroughfare given over to wildlife. But the railway bridge, over
which you walk, is still intact, and offers a pleasant view either side
down along the cutting.

Through a gate the lane continues, winding across the field until it
reaches another gate. Through this you reach the church. And what
a lovely spot this is! Now accompanied only by a farm and manor

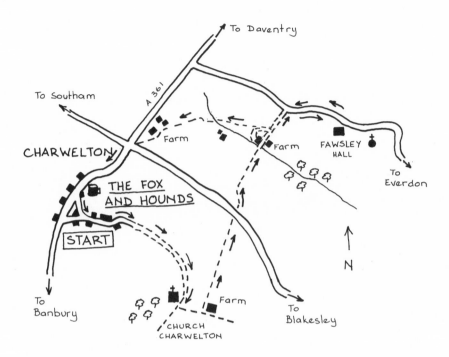

house this beautiful little 14th century church was once the centre of a thriving community.

The circular walk now continues across the field on the far side of the church. An arrow disc, nailed to a wooden post, points the way. Aim towards the farm buildings on the far side. There you will find a gate and another arrow disc pointing ahead, through the farmyard. But you do not follow this direction. Instead, turn left along a gravel trackway. This leads to another gate, on the far side of which an earth and grass way leads across a field northwards to a road. This rutted path is in fact a bridleway, and is signposted as such where it meets the road.

Through a gate on either side, cross over this road and continue in the same direction as before. The bridleway leads up to a pair of gates close together, which take you through the hedgerow, and then up to the skyline alongside a hedge on your right. Badby Down can now be seen on the distant horizon ahead – the views all round have now begun to open out. Keeping to the top of the field, with a shallow valley parallel and down to the left, you eventually reach a gate leading on to a gravel track. Continue straight on along this track, as it dips down to the farm and up the other side. In due course you reach the

Houses in Charwelton.

road. Turn right to Fawsley. Those wishing to shorten the route, and miss Fawsley, should walk only a little way beyond the farm, for the return journey starts from there.

Fawsley Hall was the home of the Knightley family from the 15th to the 19th century. It is a fine Tudor/Jacobean building. The estate was landscaped by Capability Brown, and boasts some beautiful stretches of water.

Retrace your steps to the farm you passed earlier. Just to the north of that farm, on the right as you approach from the Fawsley road, is a gate. This is not the gate you came through on your outward journey, nor the one next to it, leading to a track dipping down to some barns. It is the one that leads through to the field. Aim diagonally across this field, aiming for the distant telegraph tower on the far horizon. Keep the stream, and its valley, down to your left.

On the far side continue through a gate opening, past a pond and a group of trees and on upwards, by now keeping the stream close to your left. Up on the hill to your left is a farmstead. After about 200 yards cross the stream (which is usually dry in summer) and follow the hedge for about 50 yards, until you reach a pair of gates on the right. These lead you through the hedgerow. On the other side turn left and follow the field edge up to the farm on the skyline, keeping the fence to your left. Skirt all the farm buildings (to the left) and by way of several gates find the path that leads diagonally down across the fields.

The telegraph tower should now be half-right on the skyline. A further gate and stile now lead into the last field, in the bottom corner of which is the gap in the hedge that takes you out to the main road. Turn left to return to the Fox and Hounds.

Places of interest nearby

Canons Ashby House stands 4 miles to the south-east, and a fine manor house it is to be sure. Now owned by the National Trust it dates back to the 16th century, on a site once occupied by an Augustinian priory. The formal gardens have been lovingly restored. Refreshments are available and facilities are provided for the disabled. For those more interested in the natural environment, there are the *Badby Woods*, 2 miles away north-eastwards. East of Preston Capes (3 miles south-east of Charwelton) is the *High Wood Nature Reserve* managed by the Northamptonshire Wildlife Trust.

Braunston
The Old Plough

4

Once a coaching inn this pub is now popular amongst the boating fraternity, for the canal is not far away. The reasons for its popularity are a friendly atmosphere, a good choice of real ales and an excellent menu. There is a large garden at the rear, pub games are provided and families are welcome.

There are two separate entrances, one to the public bar off which is the skittles area (doubling as a family room), and one to the lounge. The latter room is divided up into sections by screens, the space at the back being more of a dining area (also where families tend to sit). All is dark and cosy. There is a lot of woodwork, bare stone walls and cushioned seating. The walls are hung with plates, horse-brasses and lamps. Open fires burn in winter months.

Real ales on offer include Bass and Ansells; Taunton draught cider is served, and a range of house wines. But it is the food that brings in the customers. The printed menu lists a comprehensive range of meals. From appetisers and 'plough platters' (including soups, pâté, cheese or ham salads and prawn specials), to sandwiches and 'hot platters' (including steaks, fish, sausages and burgers) there should be something for everybody. Vegetarians could have a lentil crumble or

a mushroom and nut fettucine and children have their own menu. The Old Plough keeps normal pub opening times.
Telephone: 01788 890000.

How to get there: Braunston will be found just 3 miles north-west of Daventry, close to the A45 main road to Coventry. It stands near the border with Warwickshire, in the hilly country that forms the continuation of the Cotswolds (which are further south). The Old Plough is near the church, at the western end of the village.

Parking: There is a pub car park.

Length of the walk: 2½ miles. OS Landranger map 152 Northampton and Milton Keynes. (inn GR 538662).

This is a walk for canal lovers. Braunston is an important centre for narrow boat enthusiasts: the Grand Union Canal meets the Oxford Canal, there is a large marina here, sundry boat yards and boat shops, and Braunston Lock flight carries the waterway up a 30 foot rise through six locks towards the Braunston Tunnel.

The route involves a walk across fields to the towpath, a canal-side stroll past moored narrow boats, and a return by country lane and tarmac paths. Those with prams and wheelchairs may wish to drive to the marina and park there, in order to reach the main areas of interest.

The Walk
Turn right outside the Old Plough and right again immediately before the church, taking the narrow tarmac path that runs down the edge of the graveyard. This leads past a house (on the right) which has been converted from an early 19th century windmill. The church to your left was constructed in Victorian times. At the end of the tarmac path, on Church Road, turn left and almost immediately right through a gate on the other side. There is a stile here also, and a footpath signpost.

The path across the fields to the canal is well-worn and easy to follow – and the canal itself can be seen ahead and below the whole way. Aiming diagonally across the first field (past the edge of a small cemetery) you will find two more stiles leading into the next field. Crossing the corner of this, and then bearing right down the edge of the third field (after another stile) will bring you to a grass-topped bridge. The canal is now below. Climb down the embankment and follow the towpath southwards, keeping the canal itself to your left.

The walk across the fields is very pleasant. Those wishing to miss this section, and in so doing reduce the length of the circular walk, may prefer to follow Braunston High Street all the way from the Old Plough to the canal, bearing left soon after passing the church.

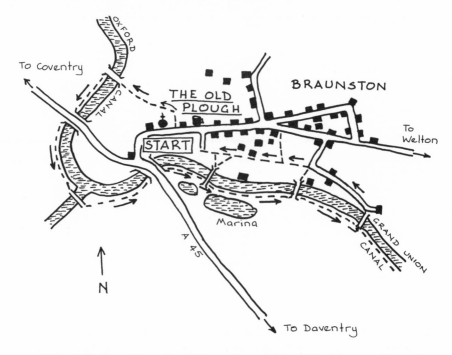

The walk along the towpath is extremely pretty. For 1½ miles you accompany narrow boats and other pleasure craft. At first you follow the Oxford Canal, along the arm that heads up to Coventry, but after the junction, you follow the Grand Union Canal. At the point where the two canals meet is a pair of elegant iron bridges. Having crossed both iron bridges continue along the towpath. The Boatman Hotel will be seen on the far bank and – beyond the next bridge over the canal – the Stop House will be passed on the near bank. The latter is a British Waterways information and exhibition centre. Further on you walk alongside the marina, which you see to your right through the bushes.

The footbridge across the mouth of this marina, which you cross soon after the Stop House, marks the spot where the Oxford Canal used to join the Grand Union – before the 1830s when the junction was moved to its present location. The towpath walk continues over a narrow wooden footbridge, past the old Pump House and on to Bottom Lock. This is the beginning of the Braunston Lock flight, along which six separate locks raise the canal by 10.8 metres. Nearby are various workshops, servicing narrow boats and canal machinery. Beyond here the towpath becomes narrower, and less suited to wheeled traffic (like cycles and prams).

24

The Oxford Canal.

At the second of the six locks is the Admiral Nelson pub. At this point you leave the towpath and start the return walk to Braunston. Cross over the bridge and follow the tarmac lane back along the north side of the canal, through the farming hamlet of Little Braunston. This is Dark Lane, and will take you all the way back to Braunston itself. Those wishing to take a more scenic route back should leave the lane at the point where it turns sharply right. A footpath continues from here across fields and through a number of kissing gates. Aim diagonally across these fields aiming for the houses in the distance and keeping the canal down to the left. In due course the path becomes a tarmac alleyway, running alongside some back gardens. Eventually, beyond some bungalows and past some garages, you emerge at the bottom of Nibbits Lane. Turn right to reach the High Street and the Old Plough.

Places of interest nearby

The town of *Daventry* is just 3 miles away to the south-east. Despite much rebuilding and redevelopment, there still remains a selection of interesting and historic buildings. The 18th century Moot Hall contains a museum. The countryside and villages north of Braunston are quiet and attractive. At *Ashby St. Ledgers* is a manor house designed by Edwin Lutyens (set behind a Tudor gatehouse and incorporating Jacobean portions).

⑤ Greens Norton
The Butchers Arms

This was built during the 1930s, after the previous pub had been damaged by fire, but a traditional style was happily maintained. Inside there are panelled walls, with high-level plate racks, beamed ceilings and brick surround fireplaces. All is very cosy and pleasant – and very welcoming.

There are two rooms, both large: a public bar with space for a pool table and darts, and a lounge which is quiet and comfortably furnished. It is in the lounge, of course, where families tend to sit. Outside there is a pleasant little garden.

This Courage pub maintains normal pub opening times. Real ales include Hook Norton, Wadworth's 6X and Directors, draught cider is Scrumpy Jack or Red Rock. The wine list includes both foreign and fruit wines. But it is the food that takes pride of place, for its range and value. There are bar snacks (ploughman's lunches, burgers, etc.), main meals (beef and ale pie, steak, scampi, ham, salads, etc.) and vegetarian dishes (like lasagne). The speciality of the house, however, are the pizzas. These are made to order, offer a selection of sizes and toppings, and are truly delicious.

Telephone: 01327 350488.

How to get there: Greens Norton is just 2 miles north-west of Towcester, and one mile west of the A5. Northampton is 9 miles away to the north-east. The village can most easily be reached from the A5–A43 roundabout, on the Towcester bypass. The Butchers Arms stands in the centre of Greens Norton, down the hill from the church.

Parking: The pub has its own car park. Vehicles can also be left in the village side streets, where space permits. There are many side streets to choose from, so parking should not be a problem.

Length of the walk: 4 miles (or shorter option). OS Landranger map 152 Northampton and Milton Keynes (inn GR 668498).

Greens Norton is an excellent centre for walks: to the north runs the Knightley Way, long distance footpath to Badby; to the south runs the Grafton Way, long distance footpath to Cosgrove. Both have been set up by Northamptonshire County Council and have proved very popular. In addition, all the local footpaths around Greens Norton have been well signposted, even to the extent that arrow discs indicate their council numbers – RN18, RN20 and so on. To the south of the village is the Greens Norton Pocket Park, an area preserved in its natural state for the enjoyment of locals. The following route passes through a section of the Pocket Park, goes around Kingthorn Wood and returns along a stretch of the Grafton Way. The paths are clear and the views are pretty. There are some stiles but few slopes to encounter.

The Walk
From outside the Butchers Arms turn right, and then right again up Bradden Road. This is opposite the general stores and is signposted to Bradden and Slapton. Just 50 yards up here on the left, clearly signposted, is a footpath. Take this. It is a clear path, and very dry because it is in fact surfaced with tarmac. It runs up beside a fence. Follow this path across the estate road and on beside another fence until it ends at a stile. Beyond are a number of horse paddocks. Walkers are reminded that horses are sensitive creatures.

The path across the paddocks, and over the intervening stiles, is clearly marked by arrow discs. It runs diagonally in a southerly direction until joining a bridleway that comes down from the right, beside a fence. At this point you bear slightly left to follow the bridleway which runs as a gravel track past Bengal Cottages. Beyond these another junction is reached. Turn right along a concrete drive, in the direction indicated by the bridleway signpost. As this concrete drive subsequently bears left into a field continue straight on (to the right) along an earthy trackway hemmed in by hedges. On the far side of the gate, that you reach shortly, is Greens Norton Pocket Park.

The route actually runs straight from this point, along the edge of

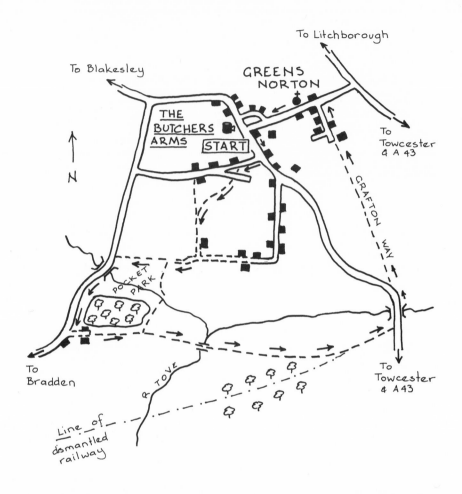

the trees, through another gate and then along the side of a field (with the hedgerow to your left) until you reach the road. However, with the Pocket Park to your left, and numerous little footpaths running down across the meadow grasslands and through patches of woodland, you may feel tempted to detour. Across the field, that you cross before the road, you should also notice the signs of ridge-and-furrow and other grassy undulations. There is a medieval landscape underneath.

On the road, turn left to follow it round a couple of bends and alongside Kingthorn Wood, which can be seen to the left. In due course, this road bends right, close to a bungalow. Before that bungalow turn down the gravel track, that leads off to the left to some

The village of Greens Norton.

farm buildings. Between the barns a gate leads through to a field. Continue in the same direction (that is, eastwards) along the edge of the field. Kingthorn Wood should still be to your left. In due course you reach the end of the wood, and a stile presents itself in the fence on the left. You now have a choice. To shorten the circular walk, cross this stile and – keeping the trees to your left – follow the path that leads directly back to Greens Norton, across the fields. To continue the route as planned, ignore the stile and maintain your easterly direction, keeping the hedgerow to your left.

This is a lovely walk across broad pastures, with views either side across the Tove meadows. In the far corner a long, narrow wooden footbridge carries you across the river Tove itself, but a metal handrail is there to steady your balance. On the far side an arrow disc points right, but another right-of-way goes straight on. Take this, cutting across diagonally to the far corner of the field, where a stile awaits. By this time you have joined a line of bushes and trees, which has appeared from the right. Across the stile you follow this line of trees, on your right. In fact, this is not simply a line of trees. It is the remnant of an old railway line. This was once part of the Stratford-upon-Avon and Midland Junction Railway, opened in 1873. At about the point where the line of trees ends, and the course of the railway seems to disappear, a further stile takes you across into the next field. This is a very large field. In the far corner a gate will lead you out onto the road.

At the road turn left, cross the bridge back over the river Tove and bear right along a footpath at the point where the road swings left. The footpath signpost here indicates a route across a little footbridge. Henceforward the journey is easy, for it follows the Grafton Way across two large fields all the way back to Greens Norton. The path is well-worn and the church spire rises above the trees directly ahead. There are a couple of little footbridges to cross and, towards the end, a couple of stiles to climb but there should be no trouble finding the way. Beyond an allotment you follow a housing estate road and turn left at the T-junction. With the church on your right, the Butchers Arms will be seen at the bottom of the hill.

Places of interest nearby

Near Tiffield, just 2 miles away north-eastwards, is the *Ark Farm Sheep Dairy*. This 100 acre farm rears animals in a traditional way and demonstrates sheep milking. Sheep dairy products are also sold. West of Greens Norton, 5 miles away at Adstone is *His Masters Shoot*, a clay pigeon shoot where professional tuition is offered. Beyond Adstone, a further 2 miles, is *Canons Ashby House*, a National Trust property.

(6) Paulerspury
The Barley Mow

A traditional village pub this, with low beams, bare stonework, alcoves, wooden furniture, brassware on the walls and a cosy, friendly atmosphere. Families are welcome, a good range of food and drink is offered, and normal pub opening times are kept. In winter months a fire burns in the large stone fireplace.

This inn first opened its doors in 1740, 21 years before William Carey – the famous missionary – was born in the village. At that time Paulerspury was still an isolated settlement standing at the edge of Whittlewood Forest. Nearby, the A5 was still an earthy thoroughfare known by its original name of Watling Street (this being a Roman road). It was to be another half century before Thomas Telford was to upgrade and resurface it. In those days the Barley Mow served thirsty farmers and foresters; today it welcomes customers from much further afield.

This pub serves various real ales, including Tiger, Ruddles and Webster's, and two draught ciders, Red Rock and Strongbow. Excellent value bar snacks and meals are offered – ploughman's lunches, rolls, things with chips, burgers, salads, fish dishes and pies for example – whilst vegetarians are suitably catered for. The front entrance leads into the main bar room, beyond which is a darker, more separate area, where hangs the dartboard. There is also a garden at the back.

Telephone: 01327 811260.

How to get there: Paulerspury is just 3 miles south-east of Towcester, down the A5 road to Milton Keynes (which is 9 miles away). It is 10 miles south of Northampton. The Barley Mow stands at the western end of the village, not far from the church.

Parking: The pub has its own car park. Vehicles can also be left along the village streets, for there is little traffic and the lanes are fairly wide.

Length of the walk: 3 miles (or shorter option). OS Landranger map 152 Northampton and Milton Keynes (inn GR 718455).

This area – once the northern fringe of Whittlewood Forest, an ancient hunting estate – is now farmed. The fields are hedged and pleasantly undulating; the views are open but not wide-ranging. And through this landscape numerous little streams have cut shallow valleys, thus providing hidden corners where the wildlife is rarely disturbed by walkers.

This circular walk takes in Pury End, an attractive hamlet west of Paulerspury. Before that settlement, clear, much-used paths are followed, across an open fieldscape. After it, lesser-known paths are followed, along a beautiful little valley. A number of stiles are encountered, and a couple of wooden footbridges, but nothing is too difficult.

The Walk

From the Barley Mow turn left, up the High Street and left again at Church Green (before the right bend and the church itself). This triangular green is surrounded by old stone cottages and is very attractive. It once formed the village centre, before the settlement spread eastwards in medieval times to link up with Watling Street (now the A5) at Plumpton End, which was once a separate hamlet. Pury End, west of Paulerspury, is still a separate hamlet, as shall be seen later. Paulerspury, and its accompanying hamlets, was once famous for its lace making, especially during the 19th century. Queen Victoria is said to have admired the intricate designs.

From Church Green keep to the right, along Park Lane, that runs past a thatched cottage. This is signposted as a dead end and a notice reads 'Private Drive to Park Farm House', just as you leave the village. Continue nevertheless, for a footpath arrow disc confirms that it is a right-of-way for walkers. It is a tarmac drive and leads straight to Park Farm across the fields. Pury End can be seen clearly to the right, across

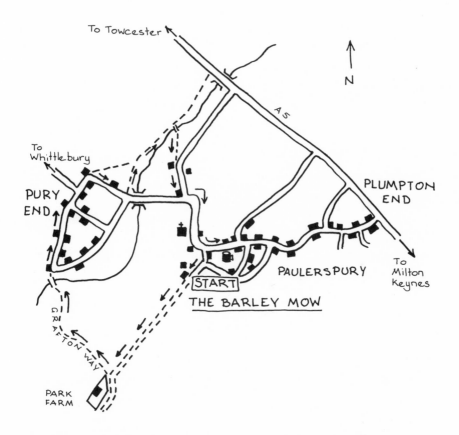

the valley. Immediately before the farm however, turn right where there is a stile, a gate and a Grafton Way indicator board. The path leading down into the valley towards Pury End, as part of the Grafton Way, is clear and well signposted. It runs down the edges of two fields (with the hedgerow to the left), bears right with the corner of the second field and then dips down to cross a narrow footbridge. On the far side you bear right, to walk up to the road and Pury End. This is a pleasant section, and an historic one. Up to the middle of the 19th century this part of the Grafton Way was a road leading into Whittlewood Forest: as you enter Pury End you should notice that the path has been entrenched into a 'hollow way' such was its former use.

Walk up the lane through Pury End, keeping left at the fork, along Careys Road. Beyond Manor Farm (on the left) ignore both Scriveners Lane on the right and the road to Whittlebury on the left. Continue past the old stone cottages to the far end where the road bends right.

Houses in Pury End.

At this point you could climb the stile that you see in front, 10 yards to the right of the gate in the corner, and then walk diagonally across the field to the half-right. This will take you down into the valley. But it would be easier to continue along the road (now heading south-eastwards), past a cottage called 'Hillcrest' and then through the gate on the left opposite the turning that cuts back to Pury End. This will take you along the side of the valley. Those wishing to shorten the circular walk should keep to the road all the way back to Paulerspury.

This last section, along a valley running northwards, is very pretty indeed. It is very quiet; the paddocks and meadows are very lush; the thickets are alive with wildlife. From the road, contour along a grassy path to a stile and thence onward across two more fields to a footbridge that takes you across a ditch and through a hedgerow. By this time you have come closer to the stream, whose valley you are following down. The next field is long and you should notice, across it, the faint signs of ridge-and-furrow, indicating former strip cultivation. Halfway across this long field, to the right, is a step stile leading to a wooden footbridge across the stream. A metal handrail will help you across. On the far side climb the grassy slope at an angle (half right) to the skyline. On the far side of this field a long stile straddles a double wooden fence. Once over this you aim for the top corner of the next field, where you will find a gate and stile to the left of a wooden stable block. The road is thus reached, opposite Cuttle

Mill Nursery. Turn right to return to Paulerspury, keeping left at the T-junction to pass the church. The Barley Mow is just around the corner.

Places of interest nearby

Towcester, which is 2 miles north-west of Paulerspury, is a town of Roman origin, standing astride Watling Street (now the A5). It has many old buildings, a modern leisure centre and, at its eastern edge, a racecourse holding several National Hunt meetings each year. Racing of a different kind can be seen regularly at Silverstone, 4 miles south-west of Paulerspury. A mile south of the Stoke Bruerne canal centre are the *Stoke Park Pavilions*, 3 miles north-eastwards. Said to have been designed by Inigo Jones, these once formed part of a great Palladian manor house, built in the 17th century. Further afield, 6 miles south-westwards, across the Buckinghamshire border, is Stowe. Here, the landscaped gardens surrounding the famous public school are owned by the National Trust and should not be missed.

Cosgrove
The Navigation Inn

This has been an inn since the early 19th century, but the building probably goes back to the late 18th century. It is thought it was originally constructed as a warehouse along the newly dug Grand Junction Canal (now the Grand Union). Today, however, the Navigation Inn offers a modern welcome in plush surroundings, where only the photographs and prints hung around the walls indicate the pub's past life.

It is a long building, split lengthways. The main door opens into the saloon bar. To the right is the Piano Bar which leads out to a balcony. The Piano Bar is especially popular at weekends when live music is provided – the room boasts a grand piano and visiting guest pianists. Throughout the pub the decor can be described as new traditional, with oak furniture, open fires and ceiling beams.

Keeping normal pub opening times, this freehouse is geared up for the canal trade. No fewer than six real ales are usually offered, including Wadworth's 6X, Craftsman and Old Speckled Hen. Scrumpy Jack draught cider is sold and a full wine list helps to tempt the drinker. The food on offer must be seen to be believed, both in variety and quality. Two large menu cards, with regular dishes, are supplemented by a blackboard that lists a dozen or so daily specials. There are sandwiches (plain and toasted), ploughman's lunches, salads, grills, fish dishes, lasagnes, things with chips and a choice of several vegetarian meals, like mushroom Stroganoff. And since the Navigation Inn welcomes families there is a children's menu also – so no one should go hungry.

Telephone: 01908 543156.

How to get there: Cosgrove is very close to the Buckinghamshire border, just a couple of miles from the northern edges of Milton Keynes. It is 12 miles south of Northampton, a little to the east of the A508 road. It can be reached easily from the A5 roundabout at Old Stratford. The Navigation Inn actually stands outside Cosgrove village, at Thrupp Wharf, one mile northwards, along the Grand Union Canal.

Parking: There is a large car park behind the pub. On the road that passes alongside there are some lay-bys. Otherwise few parking spaces present themselves. The circular walk could begin in Cosgrove with the Navigation Inn acting as a halfway staging post. In this case, cars can be left in the village.

Length of the walk: 2 miles. OS Landranger map 152 Northampton and Milton Keynes (inn GR 788436).

This pleasant little stroll offers views across the meadows of the river Great Ouse which, along this stretch, forms the boundary between Northamptonshire and Buckinghamshire. Considering how close Milton Keynes is situated, the countryside is surprisingly unspoilt. The route runs along the towpath of the Grand Union Canal, through the pretty village of Cosgrove and back along a bridleway across farmland. Throughout, the paths are clear and well signposted. There are no stiles to climb, only gates to open and close. The walk can therefore be enjoyed by everyone.

The Walk

The Navigation Inn, as the name suggests, stands against the canal – so the towpath should not be hard to find! Follow this southwards, keeping the waterway to your left. The distant spire, rising up above the trees on the far horizon, on the left, belongs to Hanslope church.

As you leave Thrupp Wharf behind so the number of boats moored diminishes, giving more chance of some wildlife sightings. Herons are common hereabouts, but kingfishers less so. In due course you come to a classical-style bridge, crossing the canal with a broad pointed arch. Here is Cosgrove. The bridge was built to match the architecture of nearby Cosgrove Lodge, whose estate has now been converted into a leisure park. Sadly the Lodge itself has gone, but it must once have

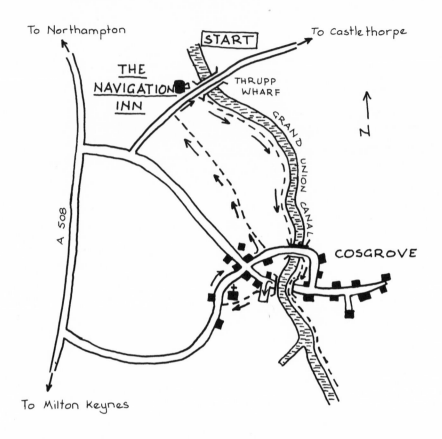

been a fine building if this bridge is anything to go by.

Cross the bridge and continue along the towpath, this time with the canal to your right. There is now a bustle of narrow boats, for this is Cosgrove Marina. There are some marine workshops here and, along the opposite bank, is the popular Barley Mow pub, with its gardens stretching down to the waterside. The route now leaves the canal: walk down the steps on the left and take the horse-shoe shaped tunnel underneath, emerging with the Barley Mow on your right.

Those with an interest in canals may care to continue along the towpath for another half mile, and then return the same way. This will allow them to see the remnants of the old canal arm that led to Old Stratford, and further on, the splendid aqueduct that carries the Grand Union over the Great Ouse river. This was built in 1811 and consists of a 101 foot long cast iron channel known as the Iron Trunk.

From the Barley Mow turn left up the gravel track opposite, beside

Bridge over the Grand Union Canal at Cosgrove.

some houses. Then, almost immediately, turn right along a narrow tarmac path that runs along beside those houses. Through a kissing gate halfway you emerge into the churchyard at the far end. Those interested should look inside the church – it is a fine piece of Gothic architecture. On the road turn right and walk down through the village, ignoring the road that goes left and continuing straight ahead down the lane signposted as a dead end (called Bridge Road). This will lead to the elegant bridge you saw earlier, on the towpath.

Before that bridge however, as the lane bears right towards it, take the path off to the left, running between the houses. There is a bridleway sign to show you the way. The path is wide and grassy, and though it can be overgrown, is clear enough. There is a fence either side, gardens to a housing estate on the left, open fields to the right. In due course you reach a gate. The way back to the Navigation Inn is now very easy to follow. Continue straight on, along the edges of three large fields, keeping the hedgerow to your left all the way. There are a number of gates to go through but these open easily. At the far end you reach the road where you turn right.

Places of interest nearby

Mill Crook Nature Reserve, situated along the river Tove near Grafton Regis, is 3 miles north-west of Cosgrove. This is a small area of hay meadow managed by the Northamptonshire Wildlife Trust.

Bugbrooke
The Five Bells

This aptly named pub – it stands opposite the church – has gained something of a reputation for its food. The selection is imaginative and should suit all tastes, including those of exacting vegetarians. The regular items include such home-made dishes as mixed grill, steak and kidney pie, lemon sole and tagliatelle. Daily specials are listed on the blackboard, and these might include pepper steak, broccoli and cheese bake, and plaice Dieppe – plaice filled with prawns and mushrooms.

To accompany your meal you could choose a real ale – Ruddles, John Smith's or one of the guest beers, a draught cider, or one of the many wines on offer.

Despite its size this is a cosy pub. There are separate bars, beamed ceilings and the middle room is especially attractive being timber-clad throughout. At one end is the games area, with bar billiards and skittles; at the other end of the building is the dining area where customers can enjoy a non-smoking environment. Pine shelf units contain an interesting bottle collection and – during winter months – log-burning stoves give everything a warm, welcoming glow.

Families are especially welcome. The garden (which is fenced off from the car park) contains children's facilities including swings and a slide.

The Five Bells keeps normal pub opening times.

Telephone: 01604 832483.

How to get there: Bugbrooke is 5 miles south-west of Northampton and 6 miles north of Towcester. It is just over a mile south of junction 16 of the M1 motorway. The village stands between the river Nene and the Grand Union Canal. The Five Bells will be found at the western end of Bugbrooke.

Parking: The pub car park has space for 50 vehicles. Cars can also be left in the village side streets, but preferably not along the main road though, which tends to be busy.

Length of the walk: 3½ miles (longer and shorter options). OS Landranger map 152 Northampton and Milton Keynes (inn GR 674574).

The Grand Union Canal cuts through the heart of Northamptonshire, and the Nene is the county's most important river. This walk links these two waterways and thus offers some excellent meadow scenery and an abundance of lowland wildlife. The pretty village of Nether Heyford is reached by way of the canal towpath and the return is made via footpaths across the Nene flood plain. The route is clear throughout, although can be damp underfoot after a period of wet weather.

The Walk

To reach the Grand Union Canal turn right outside the Five Bells, right again along the road signposted to Nether Heyford and Weedon, and then left down a tarmac track. This is just a few yards from the end of the village and is marked by a footpath signpost. It runs down through a pair of farm gates hung on brick pillars. Very shortly you will come to the bridge over the canal. Turn right down the embankment and join the towpath.

For the next mile or so you have a splendid walk along the Grand Union, with the canal to your left and views across the Nene valley to your right. All around is rolling countryside.

This canal was built from 1796, to link London with the Midlands and Northern England. It was a great success – until 1832 that is, when the railway was built almost alongside. That took traffic away from the Grand Union, which thus entered a long period of decline. Today the canal is busy again but now mostly with pleasure craft. As you approach the bridge at Heyford you will notice many such craft moored along the far bank.

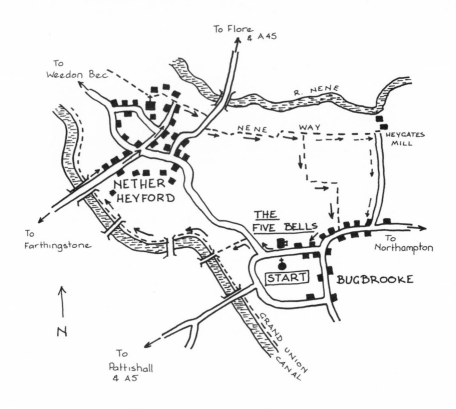

Passing under the bridge you climb the embankment to the road and walk along the pavement to Nether Heyford village centre, passing under the line of pylons on your way. At first you walk by the new houses on the outskirts but soon you reach the main village street, noting the tremendous size of the village green over to the right. Covering some 5 acres this must be one of the largest village greens in England.

The most attractive part of Nether Heyford is down by the 13th century church, which you reach by crossing the road and walking along Church Street, bearing left at the end.

The next leg of the circular walk is along part of the Nene Way. This is a long distance footpath, designated in 1990, running from Badby in the west of the county all the way to Wansford, in the north-east corner – a distance of 70 miles. The route is well signposted and well marked by regular arrow discs. Those wishing to take a shorter route back to Bugbrooke should walk along the Bugbrooke road and turn left along a footpath not far out of the village.

The Nene Way route can be picked up from behind Nether Heyford church, or else from the top end of Manor Walk, (a No Through Road to the east of the church) where you turn right. A narrow path leads along beside a high stone wall. Across the next road this footpath continues over a stile as an alley beside a brick wall. At the next road turn right and then, after about 100 yards, left along a wide gravel lane. This leads out of the housing estate and is signposted as a footpath to Kislingbury and Bugbrooke. You will notice some playing fields along here, on the left-hand side. Beyond these you reach a wide concrete bridge.

The Nene Way should be followed over the stile (half-left) and diagonally between two fields along the line of telegraph poles. Where these poles end the Way kinks left then right to continue along two more field edges, all the while keeping the hedgerow to your left. In due course you reach a stile on which are nailed two arrow discs; one pointing straight on (the Nene Way) and another one pointing right, uphill across the field. This is a moment of decision!

The longer way back to Bugbrooke, but probably the quicker since the route is simple, is to continue along the Nene Way to Heygates Mill and then turn right up Mill Lane. The shorter, but more difficult way back is to walk up the field (before crossing the stile) and then to negotiate the line of an ancient trackway. This starts from a stile, in the hedgerow that runs along the skyline. This route is clear in the sense that it is bounded on either side by a hedge but it can also be hard to follow, due to dense undergrowth. With the correct clothing and footwear it is certainly a route to be recommended – the wildlife is everywhere. The path – if it can be so described – bears left after a short while and finally ends at two farm gates. Go through the one on the right, taking a path leading southwards along a field edge. Bugbrooke church can now be seen to the half right. At the bottom of the following field you come to some farm buildings, where a kissing gate leads you round to the road. You are now back in the village. Turn right to reach the Five Bells and journey's end.

Places of interest nearby

The Old Dairy Farm Centre, at Upper Stowe (2 miles west of Bugbrooke) is a working farm with a collection of rare breeds. There is a craft centre where handmade clothes and ornaments are sold. For those interested in canals and narrow boats, both *Blisworth* and *Stoke Bruerne* should be visited. These are 4 and 6 miles to the south-east respectively. At Hunsbury Hill, on the southern outskirts of Northampton (4 miles east of Bugbrooke) is the *Northamptonshire Ironstone Railway*. There is a museum display and short train journeys are run along the old trackway on Sundays and Bank Holidays.

Boughton
The Whyte Melville

This unusual name commemorates Captain George Whyte-Melville, who lived here during the 19th century. He was a well-known author – a writer of sporting and historical novels – who gave much of his wealth to a charity that established working men's clubs. It is said that the Whyte Melville is haunted. The ghost of a young lady – who hanged herself in the upstairs sitting room – can often be heard pacing the landing.

Inside, the style has been called 'country drawing room'. The furniture is a comfortable mixture of dining tables, settles and armchairs. Areas of bare stone complement the plaster walls where old pictures are hung. The large single, open-plan bar room is subdivided by the occasional screen. There is no family room because everyone is welcome everywhere.

This is a Courage house and opens during normal pub times. The real ales offered include Pedigree, Old Speckled Hen and Boddingtons; draught cider is available and no fewer than 16 wines, all available by the glass. And the food served is excellent. Bar snacks include local pâté, steak sandwiches and Greek salads (as well as the more usual items) and main meals include various stews, casseroles, salads and grills. Vegetarians would enjoy the harvester pie, and the pub does a very good sausage speciality.

Telephone: 01604 842321.

How to get there: Boughton is almost a northern suburb of Northampton. It stands just off the A508 road that runs northwards to Market Harborough. The Whyte Melville will be found at the northern end of the village, very close to the church.

Parking: There is a large car park at the rear. Vehicles can also be left along the lanes of the village, where space permits.

Length of the walk: 3 miles (longer and shorter options). OS Landranger map 152 Northampton and Milton Keynes (inn GR 754659).

Northampton has grown rapidly over the last few decades, and continued expansion threatens to engulf Boughton. But the village remains unspoilt, and the countryside to its north remains undeveloped. The walk crosses this countryside, using public rights of way, lanes and byways. The circuit can be extended by the inclusion of Pitsford, a village standing a mile away. It can be shortened by the use of the many 'permitted' paths that wander around the fields in this area. To be seen on this walk, apart from pleasant country views, are various buildings once linked to Boughton Park.

The Walk

The northern end of Boughton is the oldest and prettiest part of the village, with honey-coloured thatched cottages, a 16th century church and a picturesque, lodged entrance to the Boughton Park estate. The Whyte Melville stands in the midst of this scene, and you can admire the charm of it all as you turn right from outside the pub and right again down Butchers Lane, which is a 'No Through Road' signposted to the village hall. At the bottom end of this lane a footpath continues, in the direction of Pitsford. The lane becomes a tarmac track, as it passes a long row of detached houses on the right, and then a gravel one as it dips down to cross a small stream.

Immediately beyond the little stone bridge that takes you over the stream bear half-left. Leaving the track, you take the stile and gate that lead into the field ahead and cross diagonally in the direction indicated by the arrow disc and signpost. Beyond the stile in the next hedgerow turn left and then right to follow the edge of the field uphill. In fact, you follow the bottom of a shallow valley northwards, all the way to the top, walking along the edge of another field as you go. The road will be found where the gradient levels off.

Those wishing to include the village of Pitsford on their circular

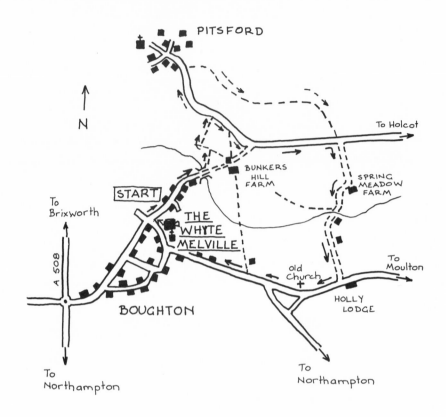

walk should turn left along the road. From Pitsford a footpath will lead them back across the fields to rejoin the 'official' route. Others should turn right along the road, and walk eastwards for about half a mile. Beyond the point where the drive to Bunkers Hill Farm leads off to the right you come to a gravel lane, also on the right. This is called Spectacle Lane and is labelled as a 'Byway'. It is opposite the footpath from Pitsford. Those who have incorporated that village on their circuit will rejoin at this point. Incidentally, there is another, shorter, way back to Boughton from the road and many may choose this. A footpath, which is signposted, leads from the old roadside quarry that you pass on your right-hand side before the Bunkers Hill Farm drive. This runs through the residential complex that is now Bunkers Hill farmstead and on to Church Furlong Farm, which stands at the eastern end of Boughton.

Spectacle Lane, a wide, hedgerow-fringed thoroughfare, leads straight to Spring Meadow Farm where it kinks right then left. Further on it curves round to a ford and footbridge, and then continues (now

The village of Boughton.

as a tarmac lane) eventually to meet the Boughton to Moulton road. What you will not fail to notice, along the stretch beyond the ford, is the tall, stone archway with turretted sides. This is a folly, and one of many erected by the Second Earl of Stratford during the 18th century. It is locally known as 'Folly Arch' or 'The Spectacles' – hence the name of this lane. Also scattered around the estate, of similar age, are an obelisk, a 'Hawking Tower' and a grand, castellated farmhouse known as Holly Lodge. The last named stands at the end of Spectacle Lane, at the point where you turn right to return to Boughton village.

Halfway back along the road, however, you should stop awhile at the ruins of Boughton's old church. It stands on the right-hand side and is surrounded by a wonderfully wild graveyard. In medieval times this was a thriving church at the centre of a thriving village. For Boughton once stood here, and the green triangle opposite the old church, now just a road junction, was the village green.

Places of interest nearby

Althorp House is only 4 miles west of Boughton. This is the 16th century home of the Earls of Spencer. Close by is *Holdenby House*, reconstructed during the 19th century from an Elizabethan foundation. The *Northampton and Lamport Railway*, near Chapel Brampton a mile westwards, preserves some buildings and rolling stock connected with the great age of steam.

10 Hackleton
The White Hart Inn

This was first recorded as an ale-house back in 1739, when Hackleton was still an isolated village set amidst the trees of Salcey Forest, at the western end of the Yardley Chase hunting estate.

The White Hart Inn is popular not just with locals but also with walkers, tourists and Northampton residents who travel here especially to enjoy its hospitality and food. There are two main rooms within, a large public bar with dartboard and Northamptonshire skittle table, and a plush lounge. The atmosphere is cosy and friendly. There are wooden beams, lots of horse-brasses hanging on the walls and – in the public bar – a fine inglenook fireplace. In the lounge an old well, said to be 40 feet deep, is set into the bar counter.

Various real ales are served at the White Hart, including Theakston's XB, Ruddles and Webster's, together with draught cider and a selection of wines. But it is the food that draws the customers. Apart from the usual snacks and meals, listed in a menu, there are various specials listed on blackboards and notices. These might include exotic spring rolls, roast pork sandwiches and – for vegetarians – spinach and cheese pancakes. The various salads, and the steak and kidney pies, are especially popular.

Normal pub opening times are kept. Children are welcome in the lounge and will enjoy the garden.
Telephone: 01604 870271.

How to get there: Hackleton is just 5 miles from the centre of Northampton, in a south-easterly direction, and 4 miles from Junction 15 of the M1 motorway. It stands on the B526 road, which links Hardingstone and Newport Pagnell. The White Hart will be found at the centre of the village, on the right as you travel from Northampton.

Parking: There is a large pub car park.

Length of the walk: 3 miles. OS Landranger map 152 Northampton and Milton Keynes. (inn GR 808550).

This is a three-village walk. Hackleton, Piddington and Horton are grouped close together just north of Salcey Forest. They are small, little known and each has its own distinctive character. This circular walk links these villages together using, for the most part, bridleways across undulating farmland. There is just one stretch of road. The route is very easy to find. Those with prams and wheelchairs may choose simply to wander around each village separately. Their lanes are quiet and their buildings are architecturally varied.

The Walk

Hackleton straddles the B526; it is linear in shape with old cottages and houses along the main road and new housing estates behind on either side. Its main claim to fame is its link with the great missionary William Carey. The walk begins close by the Carey Memorial Chapel. Turning left outside the pub and left again down The Jetty into Chapel Lane you find yourself alongside this grand red brick building. Those interested should go inside, visitors being welcome. At the bottom end of Chapel Lane a narrow path continues between hedges, with fields on either side. It is clear enough for the surface has been covered in tarmac and street lights have been erected. An easy walk even for people with prams and wheelchairs.

Beyond a little bridge this path continues straight on, eventually emerging into a modern housing estate. This is Piddington, but not the most attractive part of that village. To reach the older end continue along the street and cross the end road diagonally, taking a narrow tarmac footpath up to the church.

Piddington is a very attractive little village; very quiet and neatly maintained. From the church turn left down Church End and left again down Church Road, continuing on past the old red telephone box to the Spread Eagle pub.

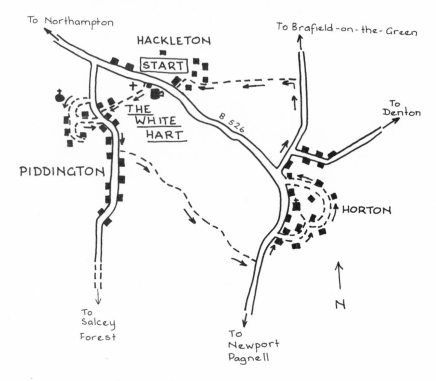

To Northampton

HACKLETON

START

To Brafield-on-the-Green

THE WHITE HART

B 526

To Denton

PIDDINGTON

HORTON

To Salcey Forest

N

To Newport Pagnell

The bridleway to Horton starts on the left-hand side of the road, opposite the Spread Eagle car park. Should you, instead, continue down the main village street you will cross an old railway line and soon find yourself on a green lane running into Salcey Forest. This village street is, you see, a cul-de-sac.

The bridleway begins as a gravel path, next to a tall coniferous hedge, but soon becomes a less clear grassy path running across the fields. But the route is never in doubt for Horton's rooftops can be seen in the distance. After the first large field you walk through a gap in the hedgerow and then along the edge of another field. Eventually you reach the road, where you turn left into the village.

Horton is an odd place! It stands to the east of the main road and consists almost entirely of modern bungalows and expensive detached houses. The roads are more like private gravel drives. Walking around, you get a very strong sense that you are trespassing. Vehicles, indeed, would be trespassing!

From the main road turn right, beside some clipped hedges. Then follow this lane round as it bears left, over a little stone bridge, then right before the church and finally left after passing in front of the

50

The Carey Memorial Chapel at Hackleton.

main block, a classical building now converted to a row of houses. Beyond the cricket pitch you emerge back on the public road, between the original lodges to the estate. This concludes an unforgettable tour around the 'village'.

The way back to Hackleton begins with a stretch of road walking. Turn right outside the lodges and walk for half a mile up Brafield Road. The bridleway, off to the left, is marked by a signpost and its route is clearly visible across the field. The spire of Piddington church can be seen in the distance ahead. Walk diagonally across two large fields, down through a hedgerow and then up through a third large field. In the far corner a small gate and stile leads through to a small paddock, where you bear right, to follow the line of some modern houses. At the end a gate leads down to a road, where you turn left to reach the B526. The White Hart will be seen to the right.

Places of interest nearby

Salcey Forest, which is 2 miles south of Hackleton, is a large area of woodland administered by the Forestry Commission. There are parking and picnic areas, numerous nature trails (including walks specially planned for woodpecker spotting), and facilities for the disabled. On the southern outskirts of Northampton, just 4 miles north-west of Hackleton, are various places to visit: *Barnes Meadow Nature Reserve, Delapre Abbey* and the *Hardingstone Eleanor Cross*.

Grendon
The Crown Inn

The pride of this pub is its selection of real ales. Being a freehouse it is able to draw its net wide – offering such beers as Marston's Pedigree, London Pride, Thwaites and Everards' Tiger. Indeed, the proprietors say that, given sufficient notice, they will get any beer for any occasion.

The choice of food is equally impressive. Listed on large menu cards the items range from jacket potatoes, sandwiches, sausages and burgers, to steaks, lemon sole, chicken Kiev and steak and kidney pie. There are chips-with-dips, chicken goujons and always something for vegetarians. Desserts include such mouth-watering temptations as chocolate fudge cake and profiteroles.

The Crown Inn is a large, handsome building, standing high above the village street. Inside there are two main bar rooms, a public bar with a pool table and a lounge. There is also a comfortable restaurant, leading off the lounge, giving customers a quiet eating area. There are beamed ceilings throughout, carpets underfoot and an open fire for the cooler months of the year.

Normal pub opening times are kept. Children are very welcome both inside and out, and there is easy access for the disabled via the

back door leading from the car park.
Telephone: 01933 663995.

How to get there: Grendon rises up above the Nene meadows, on the other side of the valley from Earls Barton. Wellingborough is 4 miles to the north and Northampton 8 miles to the west. The village is most easily approached from the A509 road, turning off at either Wollaston or Bozeat. The Crown stands at the western end, opposite the road to Castle Ashby.

Parking: The pub has its own car park. Vehicles can also be left anywhere in the village, provided no obstruction is caused.

Length of the walk: 4½ miles (or shorter options). OS Landranger map 152 Northampton and Milton Keynes (inn GR 877603).

Apart from one stretch of road – which is very quiet in any case – this walk involves footpaths and bridleways across undulating farmland. There are distant views to be enjoyed, of villages, church towers and – from time to time – of Castle Ashby House itself. The route is clearly marked throughout, with many signposts and arrow discs. There are some stiles to be climbed, and walkers are reminded to close gates behind them since much of the land is grazed by animals. The circuit takes in the Castle Ashby estate and the little village of Easton Maudit, both well worth a visit.

The Walk
The footpath to Castle Ashby, forming the first leg of the walk, begins opposite The Crown. It will be found through a kissing gate wedged between a stone-built house and a brick-built garden wall.

From the second kissing gate 20 yards further on from the first, the views open out. A field lies ahead and below whilst in the western distance are the slopes rising to Northampton. To the half-left (in the middle distance) you can see, amongst the trees, Castle Ashby House.

The footpath runs down across the first field in the direction of Castle Ashby, diagonally over the remnants of ridge and furrow (grassy ridges indicating the old strip cultivation). At the far side is a stile, upon which an arrow disc points the way. There are some very large fields ahead. Depending upon the time of year, you may be tempted to skirt along the top edges of these fields. But the right of way in fact runs obliquely downhill, all the while in the direction of Castle Ashby. Walking under the line of pylons and through a hedgerow you will eventually meet the road. On your way you should notice the lakes down to your right – one of the well-known features of the Castle Ashby estate. This was landscaped in the 18th century by Capability

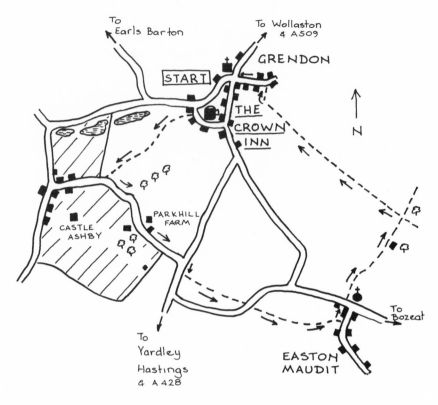

Brown who saw water as an important element in 'natural' parkland.

For the next half mile you keep to the tarmac, following the road up to the left, past Parkhill Farm, and then turning right at the T-junction. Over the estate boundary (on the right) you catch occasional glimpses of the House, to the left and straight on views begin to open out as you climb. The spire of Easton Maudit church can be seen rising from the trees on the skyline.

After about 100 yards from the T-junction you leave the road, taking a path on the left signposted as a bridleway. On the right, opposite this path, is a private track to one of the lodges to the estate – an attractive 'cottage ornée'. This is a cottage made to look 'quaint', here with the aid of a thatched roof.

The route to Easton Maudit is now very clear – a bridleway all the way and the church spire visible for much of the distance to the half-left. You walk across one field, over a concrete-and-metal bridge, up along the edge of another field, in due course passing beneath a line of pylons. Keeping almost a straight line you cross the road and

Easton Maudit church.

continue up along the bridleway, eventually dipping down to a farm at the southern end of Easton Maudit village. On the road turn left for the church.

The estate here was owned by the Mauduit family in the 12th century, hence the present village name. Later, in Tudor times, it was held by the Yelverton family, one of whose number, Sir Christopher, was the Speaker of the House of Commons who penned the daily prayer still used by Parliament. The old manor house stood behind the church, on a site now occupied only by some cedar trees.

The last leg of the circular walk begins next to the church, along a gravel track signposted as a footpath to Grendon and Bozeat. From the cedar trees mentioned earlier you can see the Grendon church tower to the half-left and the Bozeat church spire over to the right. Continuing down the gravel track you come to a gate. From here the path bears slightly right, running to the farm buildings you can see across the field. Beyond these farm buildings, and through another gate, the path continues, this time along the edge of a large field. Keep the little stream, and hedgerow, to your right. About half way along this stretch is a meeting of ways: a plank bridge and path to your right, other paths straight on and to the left. Arrow discs show the directions. Choose the left turn, and cross the field, heading directly towards Grendon, visible on the skyline.

The route now is direct and easy to find. The path crosses several fields diagonally and then, beyond a plank bridge over a ditch, along field edges up towards the houses. Two more stiles take the path to the right and onto the road where you turn left. You can now wander back through Grendon to the Crown, your walk successfully accomplished.

Places of interest nearby

Castle Ashby, close by and seen from the walk, should not really be missed. Apart from the house, church and the 18th century landscaped parklands there are Victorian gardens to be seen, a rural craft centre to visit and a farm shop. For more lively pursuits there is *Billing Aquadrome* (4 miles westward near Northampton) for swimming, boating, fishing; and *Irchester Country Park* (4 miles northwards near Wellingborough) with nature trails, woodland walks and a wayfaring course.

12 **West Haddon**
The Pytchley Inn Hotel

An impressive place this, not just because of its large, classical building but also because of its hospitality, facilities and range of refreshments.

Inside, through the main entrance into the reception area, turn right to reach the main bar room. There you will find a dark, cosy, friendly atmosphere. Large hunting pictures decorate the walls and a high shelf around the room is bedecked with plates and brassware.

This is a freehouse serving real ales including John Smith's and Directors, draught cider and an extensive range of wines. The large regular menu is supplemented with daily specials written up on a blackboard. Bar snacks include burgers, jacket potatoes, pâté, stuffed mushrooms and ploughman's lunches; main meals include various steaks, grills and fish dishes. There are moussakas and lasagnes, vegetarian bakes, several children's items (mostly things with chips) and a selection of sweets. All the food is well presented and reasonably priced.

The pub has the added advantage of being open every day from 12 noon to 11 pm (except Sundays when normal times are kept). Children are welcome – there is a family room – and a pleasant beer garden is situated outside.

Telephone: 01788 510426

How to get there: West Haddon stands at a road junction, where the A428 Rugby to Northampton road crosses the B4036 Daventry to Market Harborough road. It is in the north-west of the county, 8 miles west of Brixworth, 3 miles north of Long Buckby. Junction 18 on the M1 motorway is just 4 miles westward, beyond the village of Crick. The Pytchley Inn will be found at the eastern end of West Haddon, on the A428.

Parking: There is a large pub car park. Cars can also be left elsewhere since, throughout West Haddon, there are spaces for vehicles along the roadsides. The lanes however, may prove easier to use than the A428, which can be busy.

Length of the walk: 4 miles. OS Landranger map 140 Leicester and Coventry (inn GR 629718).

This walk is to Winwick and back. The outward journey involves a 'gated road', a narrow tarmac lane along which vehicles are seldom seen. The return journey is by bridleway and footpath, both clearly marked as they cross the undulating farmlands. Winwick is a small settlement consisting of a few cottages, some farms, a manor house and a church. Those pushing wheel or pushchairs could do worse than just walk to Winwick and back along the gated road. This would have a distance of about 2½ miles in all.

The Walk

By turning right outside the Pytchley Inn (along the A428), right at the northern edge of West Haddon, along the lane signposted to Yelvertoft and Winwick, and then, very shortly, right again you reach the gated road. It is signposted as 'Unsuitable for Through Traffic'.

This way to Winwick, of course, needs no description. It is tarmac all the way. There are four gates in all to go through but the first is usually kept open. The total distance is about a mile. All that needs be said is that the views are splendid either side.

At Winwick you reach a junction of lanes, and a directional signpost. On one corner is an attractive thatched cottage. The ways straight on and right are 'No Through Roads' and the way left is to Crick. Take the lane that goes right unless you want to look at the church first, in which case go straight on.

Winwick must have been much larger and more important once. It stands at the junction of no fewer than five routeways, but today only one of these is a proper access road. Two are gated lanes and two are bridleways. The church is 13th century and the manor house is 16th century. During the 15th century the Lord of the Manor here was Sir Thomas Malory, author of *Le Morte d' Arthur* one of the

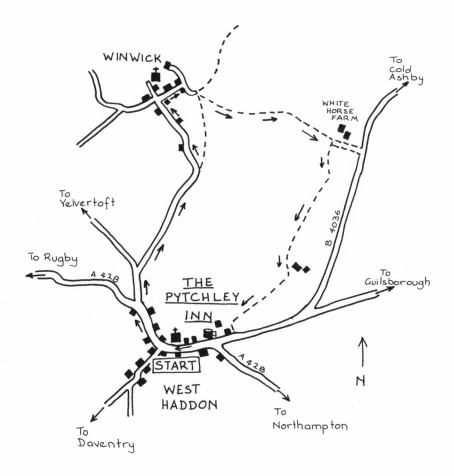

first books to be printed by William Caxton.

Having turned right at the thatched cottage you follow the lane past the entrance to Winwick Hall and the brick-built Rectory Cottage. After bearing right you soon reach a gate on the left and, seemingly, the end of the lane. Ahead is a footpath through some bushes, signposted to West Haddon. Do not follow this. Instead go through the gate and bear right, along a clear trackway that runs down the edge of the field, with the hedgerow to the right. The other track that leads uphill, with the hedgerow to the left, leads to Cold Ashby and should not be followed.

The bridleway that you do follow runs eastward across a number of fields and through a number of gates. It is not totally clear throughout its length but the route is nevertheless obvious. In an almost straight

Winwick House.

line it runs up a slight hill and down the other side, for a long stretch keeping close to a hedgerow which is on the right. Beyond a stream, which you cross in the valley, you climb along by a hedge on your left to a further gate, on the far side of which the track becomes clearer again. It runs between hedgerows some 20 yards apart. Near the top of the hill, where White House Farm will be seen on the left, you reach a gate. On the other side of this turn right immediately, to another gate. An arrow disc here points the way ahead.

The footpath back to West Haddon crosses farmland in a south-westerly direction, roughly parallel to the B4036 which is several hundred yards over to the left. There are several stiles to climb, many of which have arrow discs nailed up to show the way. All the while there are views to the right, across the hills into Leicestershire and Warwickshire. After crossing the middle of the first two fields, bear slightly right and cross the next two fields diagonally, down into a small valley. At the bottom of this, cross over a rivulet and aim up along the edge of the next field to a small, corrugated-iron, barn, which you reach on your left-hand side. Next to this barn do not continue along the gravel track ahead. Instead turn right, passing through the hedgerow using two stiles and a plank bridge over a ditch. At the far side you emerge into an enormous field. Keeping the hedgerow to your right continue along the edge of this field. West Haddon will soon be seen clearly ahead, on the distant skyline. The route is almost dead straight. Along by the hedgerow you come eventually to a small brick barn – making sure the hedgerow is still to your right after a wide gap along its length. Further on still you reach the housing estate for which you have been aiming. Through a gap in a wire fence you turn left for the road. This is the eastern end of West Haddon. Turn right and walk back to the Pytchley Inn, along the B4036.

Places of interest nearby

Coton Manor Garden, which is 3 miles east of West Haddon, is open three afternoons a week throughout the summer. Nearby is *Cottesbrooke Hall*, 5 miles from West Haddon. This elegant Queen Anne mansion is said to have inspired Jane Austen's *Mansfield Park*. *Naseby Battlefield and Museum* will be found 4 miles north-east of West Haddon. A monument marks the field where the battle took place and there is a museum in the village.

13 Arthingworth
The Bull's Head Inn

This has become a very popular pub – it is very friendly, sells a wonderful range of food and drink and is open every day from lunchtime to 11 pm. Teas, coffees and snacks are always available; children are very welcome, and set-menu lunches offer excellent value.

Inside there is, technically, one main bar room. But this is so large, and so divided by walls, steps and corners, that the impression is of many different rooms. One section acts as a public bar, with pub games, another section as a lounge-cum-dining area. Round the side is another space, which is quieter and darker than the rest. The decor is a happy clutter, with farm implements, plates and brassware adorning the walls.

As a freehouse, the Bull's Head has positively spread its wings when it comes to the real ale choice – Boddingtons, Hook Norton, Speckled Hen and so on. The regular food menu showing the usual pub fare, is supplemented by a blackboard list of specials, that might include steaks, fish dishes, chilli, seafood platters and such like. There is also plenty of choice for vegetarians – a mushroom and walnut Stroganoff for example, or vegetable curry. The desserts are equally

wide-ranging – puddings, ices, fruits, cakes, etc.
Telephone: 01858 525637.

How to get there: Arthingworth is just 3 miles south of Market Harborough and the Leicestershire border. Rothwell and Desborough are 4 miles away to the east, Brixworth is 9 miles to the south. The village is most easily reached from the A508 and A14 roads, leaving each at Kelmarsh (close to which is the main junction). The Bull's Head stands at the southern end of Arthingworth, close to the church.

Parking: There is a car park attached to the pub. Vehicles can also be left, where space allows, along the village streets. Oxendon Road, along which the circular walk begins, is a 'No Through Road' and thus offers the best option for car parking.

Length of the walk: 3½ miles (shorter and longer options). OS Landranger map 141 Kettering and Corby (inn GR 754813).

This walk includes a section of the Brampton Valley Way – a popular footpath and cycle route along the old railway line between Chapel Brampton and Market Harborough. The track along this stretch is wide, clear and firm and thus suitable for those pushing prams or wheelchairs. There is a choice of routes both to and from Arthingworth, connecting with the Brampton Valley Way. Walkers can select those routes best suited to their needs and to the time they have available. All the footpaths employed are clearly signposted and well-worn, even when crossing farmland.

The Walk
Turn left outside the Bull's Head, and left again along Oxendon Road. This is a 'No Through Road' and signposted to the 'Village Only'. At the far end, beyond the last houses, a number of different routes present themselves and walkers may choose their preferred path. The easiest, and shortest, route to reach the Brampton Valley Way – and the route suitable for prams and wheelchairs – is down the narrow tarmac lane. This leads across the fields and is hedgeless either side. It was once a public road used by motorised traffic but now it is only used by walkers and cyclists. A longer and prettier route – and the one recommended here – begins at the gate to the left of the tarmac lane. This is marked by a bridleway arrow disc and leads down, beside some old farm buildings. One of the two footpaths signposted at the right-hand side of the tarmac lane will be used upon your return to Arthingworth.

The bridleway begins down a wide, hedge-fringed track, earthy floored and rutted. At the bottom end this track crosses a stream and ends at a gate. Beyond, the way becomes a grassy path across fields.

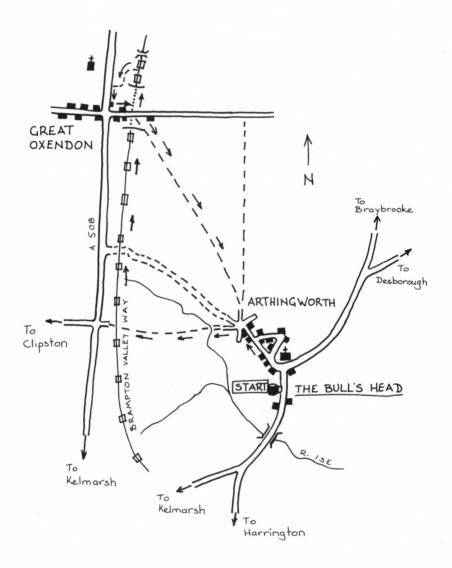

Arrow discs show the way and the route is clear. From the gate bear slightly right, to cross the field keeping the hedge to your left. Through a copse of trees you reach the far side, where another gate leads through to the next field. Continue straight on. At the distant hedgerow, through a small wooded area, a third gate takes you into the third field. With the hedge to your left follow the edge of this until you reach a pleasant little spot where an open access disc indicates

64

Great Oxendon church.

that walkers can wander at will. In front you will see the old rail bridge, over which runs the Brampton Valley Way. Gates keep animals out and these should be closed behind you. Climb up the embankment and join the Brampton Valley Way, turning right to follow it northwards.

In due course you reach the point where the tarmac lane from Arthingworth comes down to meet the Brampton Valley Way. There are more gates here, and a directional signpost. Those wishing to curtail their walk should return to the Bull's Head via the tarmac lane. Those wishing to avoid the forthcoming tunnel should turn left, join the main road (the A508) and follow that to Great Oxendon. Those wishing to continue the circuit as planned should continue along the old railway line, signposted to Market Harborough.

The Oxendon Tunnel, which you soon have to walk through, is about 400 yards long. But it is straight so you can see the light at the far end upon entering. And considering its age it is not at all damp. Merely dark. Beyond the exit, and before the next rail bridge, a flight of steps leads up the embankment on the left. Take these, to follow a path back through the sloping woodland of the cutting. On the right, opposite the end of the tunnel which is down on the left, a stile leads to a path across a field. This cuts diagonally across to a further stile, thence to the main road (just to the right of a bungalow). Turn left to walk past The George pub and reach the road junction. Great

Oxendon is along the road to the right.

The way back to Arthingworth begins a little way up the road that is signposted to Braybrooke and Desborough. The stile will be found about 100 yards along, on the right, immediately before a garage. The path (which is signposted) climbs the field to the skyline, runs past the right-hand side of the Oxendon Tunnel air shaft and then diagonally downhill. There is a view all around from this hill, and the fields all about have ridge-and-furrow markings. Ahead, and in the distance, is Arthingworth.

The route back is now almost dead straight. It runs diagonally across a number of large fields, crossing from one field to another by way of stiles or plank bridges over ditches. All the while aim for Arthingworth. The path is well-used and should be clear. In due course you arrive back at the end of Oxendon Road, from where the return to the Bull's Head is easy.

Places of interest nearby

In Arthingworth village itself are the *Coughton Galleries*, housed in the manor house near the church, with a display of 20th century British and Irish paintings. Just 2 miles away south-westwards is *Kelmarsh Hall*, a Palladian mansion designed by James Gibbs in the early 18th century. *Lamport Hall*, 4 miles to the south, dates back to the 16th century but owes its present appearance to the following two centuries when classical architecture was all the rage.

Walgrave
The Royal Oak

14

How does one begin to describe this pub? It is cosy and friendly; it offers drinkers six real ales and sixteen different wines (plus three on draught); it boasts one of the finest selections of food in the county, and it welcomes children any time both inside and out.

There has been a pub here since the early 19th century but only in recent years has the Royal Oak developed into one of the most popular hostelries in northern Northamptonshire. Inside, one large room has been divided up into separate eating and drinking areas, with the aid of wooden screens. There are bare stone fireplaces, wooden dado boards around the walls and beams hung with chinaware and mugs.

The menu is extensive with large bill-of-fare cards listing the regular items and blackboards on the walls listing the daily dishes. Amongst the former are snacks (sandwiches, jacket potatoes, burgers and such like), chef specials like steaks, beef-in-ale pies and chicken Kievs, and vegetarian meals such as tuna and tagliatelle bake, and vegetable pasties. Amongst the latter might be beef Wellington, curry, seafood salad, and quiche. If all this were not enough, at the back of the Royal Oak is a carvery restaurant offering a separate eating area.

Real ales include Boddingtons or Bateman's. Normal pub opening times are kept.
Telephone: 01604 781248.

How to get there: Walgrave lies between Northampton and Kettering, 8 miles from the former and 6 miles from the latter. It is a little to the north of Pitsford reservoir. It does not stand on a main road, but can be reached both from the A43 and the A508. The Royal Oak will be found at the eastern end of the village.

Parking: There is a pub car park for 30 vehicles. Cars are also parked in front of the Royal Oak.

Length of the walk: 2½ miles. OS Landranger map 141 Kettering and Corby (inn GR 804723).

The countryside between Kettering and Northampton has not yet been discovered – except by discerning locals. It is quiet, unspoilt and pretty, with broad undulations, a scatter of old villages and a patchwork of hedged fields. The following walk is set in the midst of this countryside and thus offers some lovely views. It links two attractive, and historic, villages by way of footpaths over rolling farmland. The route is clearly marked throughout, there being numerous signposts and arrow discs all the way. The paths are well-trodden and the ground underfoot is firm. There are, however, many stiles to climb.

The Walk

Turning right outside the Royal Oak you soon come down to the little green triangle that acts as the road junction at the centre of the village. The tall spire of Walgrave church rises up above the trees and, off to the right, is a little lane of old cottages.

Keep to the left at the triangle and then turn right up Rectory Lane. This climbs up past some interesting timber clad bungalows (on the left) and then levels off towards a bend. Before this bend, however, you will see, on the left and just past Marlowe Cottage, a footpath signpost. Climb the stile here and start to enjoy the views, for the route to Hannington now begins.

There are, in fact, two footpaths starting from the signpost. Ignore the one leading off half-right and take the one leading straight on, running alongside a garden wall. Soon this path bears slightly left and leads down to the bottom corner of the field, where you will find a gate leading on to a wooden bridge.

From the bridge take the path that leads straight up across the field, aiming for the top left-hand corner, where ends the hedgerow running along the skyline. There, a gate leads through to another field, across

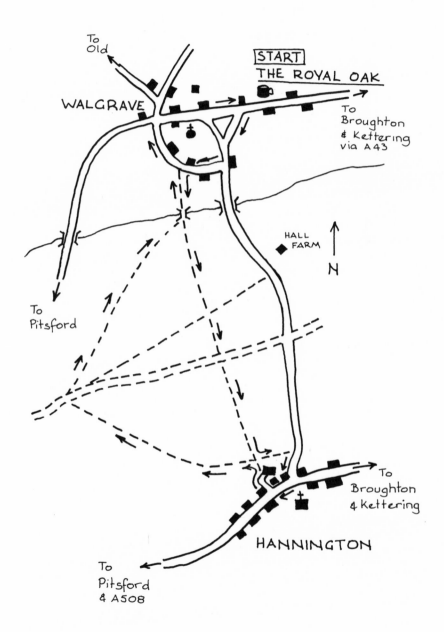

To Old

WALGRAVE

START
THE ROYAL OAK

To
Broughton
& Kettering
via A43

HALL
FARM

N

To Pitsford

To
Broughton
& Kettering

HANNINGTON

To
Pitsford
& A508

the corner of which is a stile. Over to the distant left is the northern end of Walgrave and, on the far hillside, Hall Farm. This stands close to the site of an old Tudor manor house, whose old fish ponds can still be made out in the field undulations. Beyond the stile the footpath crosses a large field, diagonally towards the left-hand end of a short line of trees.

Those trees mark the line of an old road, now reduced to an earthy, hedge-bound track. This was once part of the Brixworth to Pytchley road, a busy thoroughfare in medieval times. Cross straight over this trackway, a stile on the far side of which leads to another footpath across a field.

The way to Hannington is now clear; you can see the church tower amongst the trees in the distance. After crossing two fields (aiming directly for the church) you come to a stile set into a wooden fence. Turn left immediately after climbing this stile and follow the path that runs beside that same fence. This leads directly to the road. Turn right. Hannington is but a few steps away.

The route back to Walgrave begins next to the village hall, found at the end of School Lane, opposite Hannington church. The footpath signpost indicates the direction; through a gate and across a little valley. This first stretch may seem odd but it is a right of way. It runs between two private garden walls, across lawns and over a 'rustic' wooden bridge.

At the top of the far slope you reach the stile and wooden fence that you encountered earlier. This time do not climb over the stile but turn left, to follow the path along the fence to another stile. Now continue in the same direction (west) along the edges of two fields, keeping the hedgerow on your left. At the end of the second field turn right with the field boundary and then, after 50 yards, left across another stile. Across the next field the path runs diagonally towards the right-hand end of a group of trees.

Once again, you now cross the old road you crossed on your outward journey, but this time further along it to the west. The stiles either side of this old road are diagonally off-set. The stile on the far side of the old road has two arrow discs, showing a path to the right, and another to the half-right. Choose the latter. In fact, the choice should be obvious. The spire of Walgrave church can be seen clearly in front. The footpath runs diagonally across three fields, eventually coming down to the wooden bridge you crossed at the very start of your walk. From here you can retrace your steps back to the Royal Oak.

Hannington church.

Places of interest nearby

Just a mile outside Walgrave, on the Kettering road, is *Manvell Farm Park* where visitors can stroll around an attractively run smallholding. A mile on the other side of Walgrave is *Pitsford Water*. Fishing and sailing can be arranged there, and an information centre gives an outline of the history and facilities. Those interested in archaeology and architecture may like to go to *Brixworth* (4 miles to the west) where stands one of the finest Anglo-Saxon churches in England. *Lamport Hall*, 3 miles north-westwards, is a mansion dating back to the 16th century containing furniture and paintings.

15 Stoke Albany
The White Horse

The building is said to date from the early 18th century, but it has been a pub only since the beginning of the 20th century. Be that as it may, the interior decor and atmosphere are very traditional, if not especially old. There are bare stone walls and beams across the ceiling (complete with horsebrasses); there is a brick chimney breast and an abundance of wood panelling. The furniture includes wooden tables and cushioned bench seats.

The main entrance is round the back of the building, reached through the car park. Inside there is one large open-plan room, but this is sub-divided since it spreads across three levels. The large central area contains the bar itself and pool table. The lower level, down some steps, acts as a lounge and the upper level (at the other end) is used by some as an eating area (despite the existence here of a fruit machine). In fact, food can be consumed anywhere. And good food it is too. A full regular selection is offered and daily specials are listed on a blackboard. Snacks include bacon rolls, burgers, savoury pancakes and ploughman's lunches; main meals include various meat and fish dishes – pies, grills, salads and so on. There is, in addition, a wide range of vegetarian courses, of an imaginative nature.

This freehouse is open normal pub times. Real ales sold include Bass and Worthington. The White Horse is a friendly place where children are welcome – families normally sitting in those areas farthest from the bar.
Telephone: 01858 535268.

How to get there: Stoke Albany lies midway between Market Harborough and Corby, being 4 miles from each. It is close to the Leicestershire border. Desborough and Rothwell stand to the south, 3 and 5 miles away respectively. The village has been by-passed by the A427 road. The White Horse will be found on the road junction at the southern end of Stoke Albany.

Parking: There is a pub car park. Vehicles can also be left along the side of the road opposite the White Horse, going downhill to the church.

Length of the walk: 2 miles. OS Landranger map 141 Kettering and Corby (inn GR 807877).

This short circuit would be suitable for an evening stroll or a pre-lunch ramble. It links Stoke Albany with Wilbarston, using footpaths across farmland. Both villages are quiet, old and attractive. They have an abundance of interesting architecture and more than their fair share of history. The views to be had are good too since this is hilly countryside. The footpaths followed are generally clear, and well-trodden by locals. Some stiles are encountered but these should not cause any problems.

The Walk
Outside the White Horse turn right, not along Desborough Road which runs beside the car park, but down the old main road that is signposted to the A427 and Corby. This road bends right, then left out of the village. Where it bends left however, continue straight on, along a footpath. The stile is set high on the roadside bank, half-hidden by the hedgerow. There is a footpath signpost here, pointing the way.
    The path cuts across the middle of a field, over the brow of a hill and down across the middle of another field to a stile and wooden footbridge. The views north, from the brow of the hill, are very pleasant: rolling countryside that sweeps towards the hills of Leicestershire. The stream you cross in the valley here is a tributary of the river Welland, one of the great waterways of the Midlands. It flows eventually into the Wash. On the far side of the footbridge walk up across the field to the left of the detached house, close to which you will find a gate. On the far side is the road, and the edge of Wilbarston. To see more of the village choose the lane that goes

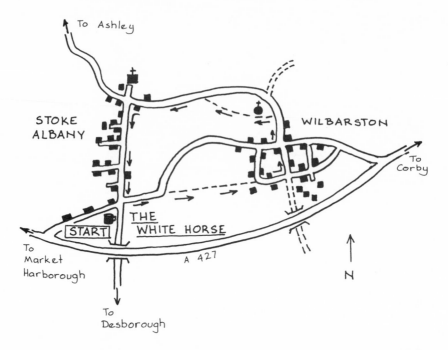

To Ashley

STOKE ALBANY

WILBARSTON

To Corby

START · THE WHITE HORSE

To Market Harborough

A 427

N

To Desborough

straight on, up the hill, as opposed to that which goes off to the left.

Past a collection of stone cottages, you arrive in due course at a junction at the top. Turn left along Rushton Road, to reach the village centre. Wilbarston is said to be named after a 7th century tribal leader called Wilbeorht, and certainly the settlement has Saxon foundations. Of the many old buildings, Pilgrim Cottage is perhaps one of the most interesting. This dates from the 17th century and is said to be haunted. Also near the village centre are the old manor house and a house formerly Dallacre Farm, each set around a courtyard.

At the crossroads, continue down the road signposted to Ashley, keeping the Fox Inn to your right. This leads to the church, on the left just before the road descends more steeply as it leaves the village.

Along the back wall of the churchyard is a kissing gate. Go through this and walk down across the field diagonally to the half-right. Down at the bottom, to the left of the far corner, a little stone bridge carries you across the stream to a stile. Cross the next field, again half-right, to a stile in the corner. This leads out onto the road where you turn left.

It is now but a short stroll to the bottom end of Stoke Albany village. Here you will find the attractive green, complete with war memorial, village hall and, behind the trees in the corner, the church. Like its

Middle Lane, Stoke Albany.

neighbouring church, this also is largely 13th century. Lord Chief Justice Denman is buried here. He was the great parliamentarian who defended Queen Caroline against King George IV, at the beginning of the 19th century.

To return to the White Horse, walk uphill from the village green. On your way you will notice, over to the right, lanes running off at right angles; Bottom Lane, Chapel Lane, Middle Lane and Green Lane. Along these are some pretty stone cottages, many of them thatched. During the 12th century the manor was held by William de Albini, after whom the village was later named. He greatly expanded the village here, laying out the roads on a grid pattern.

Places of interest nearby

The East Carlton Countryside Park, which is 2 miles away in the direction of Corby, surrounds a chateau-style mansion once owned by the Steel Corporation. North of Corby, and 5 miles north-east of Stoke Albany, is *Rockingham Castle*, which dates back to Norman times. Here there are domestic rooms on show, with painting and armour exhibits, and attractive gardens. South of Stoke Albany are three of the buildings built by Sir Thomas Tresham in the 16th century; the Market House at Rothwell, Rushton Hall and the *Rushton Triangular Lodge*, which is just 3 miles away. The three-sided building, on three floors, is a unique folly now owned by English Heritage.

⑯ Geddington
The Star Inn

This is a popular pub, and understandably so. It has a happy, friendly atmosphere, sells a wide selection of drinks and serves an excellent range of food. On top of all this it has lots of space – several different rooms, a patio at the back and tables outside at the front.

The Star Inn is a freehouse, offering at least six different real ales, including Old Speckled Hen, Abbot, Pedigree and Webster's Yorkshire. The choice of food is equally impressive. There is a standard menu, kept on the counter, together with various daily specials listed on large blackboards. You could have soups, salads, seafood platters or pâté dishes; steak and kidney pies, mixed grills or Cumberland sausages; lasagnes, chilli-con-carne or sweet-and-sour pork. Authentic Indian meals are often also offered and vegetarians are well supplied – with a pasta and bean medley perhaps or a vegetable fricassee. Desserts might include chocolate fudge cake or nutty gooseberry tart.

As you enter from the village street the public bar, with darts and skittles, is to the right, the lounge to the left. Off the latter and down some steps is a separate restaurant, and beyond the bar is a separate seating area up some other steps. The decor is traditional, with bare

76

stone fireplaces, wood-panelled ceilings and walls hung with prints. Log fires burn in winter.

The Star Inn is open throughout each afternoon, although normal pub times should be seen as the periods when food is served.

Telephone: 01536 742386.

How to get there: Geddington stands half way between Kettering and Corby, being 4 miles from the centre of each. The A43 main road runs through the western end of the village. The Star Inn will be found at the heart of Geddington, almost in the shadow of the Eleanor Cross.

Parking: The pub has its own car park. Vehicles can also be left anywhere in the village provided, of course, no obstruction is caused.

Length of the walk: 3 miles. OS Landranger map 141 Kettering and Corby (inn GR 894830).

This is a walk through history, and time should be set aside for the relaxed study of the various sites of interest passed during the circuit. Geddington has many old buildings, several of which have connections with medieval royalty, together with an elegant 13th century bridge and the well-known Eleanor Cross. Newton is the site of a lost settlement and a Tudor manor house, these now being indicated by an isolated church and a grand old dovecote. The walk involves two stretches of country lane, a clear footpath across fields and a bridleway. There are some stiles to negotiate but nothing to cause problems. Simply enjoy the views and discover something of Northamptonshire's past.

The Walk

Outside the Star Inn you cannot help but notice the Eleanor Cross, standing at the centre of the road junction. It is said to be the best preserved of the three originals that still survive, the other two being at Hardingstone and at Waltham Cross in Hertfordshire. Queen Eleanor died in 1290 at Harby in Nottinghamshire. Edward I later commemorated her death with a series of twelve crosses, each built at a place where her body rested on its journey to Westminster Abbey.

From this cross, walk south and over the double-arched medieval bridge which spans the river Ise. There is a ford here also. Continue along the village street, past numerous old stone-built cottages and, on the right, the White Lion. Towards the top end turn right along Grange Road and then across the main A43 trunk road to continue in the same direction (still along Grange Road). There is a sign indicating that the way ahead is 'Unsuitable for Heavy Goods Vehicles'. This is the way you will be walking.

For the first mile the route lies along Grange Road, which becomes

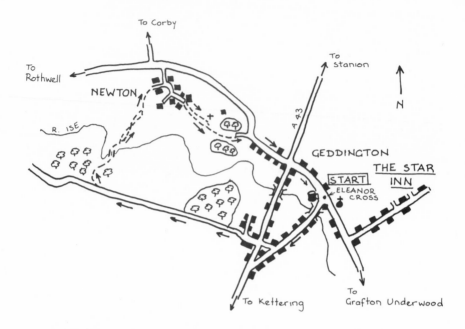

a narrow country lane soon after leaving the village. But it is not a busy
thoroughfare. In consequence you can enjoy a pleasant walk with
views on both sides. For a while a woodland to your right blocks the
view across the Ise valley. Soon, however, all is revealed – a sweep
of fields, Newton village set upon the distant slope and there, standing
alone in a field, the old church and dovecote that mark the site of a
once thriving community.

In due course the lane bends left as it approaches a second
woodland on the right. This is the point where you leave the tarmac
and head off across country. A footpath signpost points the way down
a well-trodden track that runs down towards the trees. Newton village
can be seen clearly across the valley over to the right.

The track becomes a woodland pathway, meandering between the
trees. Keep to the right, when a very tempting path leads off to the left,
and follow the route made naturally by the landscape. The earthy
bank on your right gives the impression that you are walking along a
hollow way – an ancient footpath.

At the end of the woodland a stile leads you through to a field.
Follow the direction suggested by the arrow disc, along the river bank
to a wooden footbridge. The river Ise along this section is deeply cut
down in a little gulley – so the bridge is vitally important. On the far
side bear half-right and aim for the right-hand end of the buildings of

The dovecote at Newton village.

Newton. Over the next stile you aim for the left-hand end of the buildings. This direction you now maintain over another stile, until you reach a gate. Turn right towards a thatched cottage, where you emerge into the village itself.

By walking through Newton, keeping left past a cottage called The Old Dairy and then, at the far end, turning right down a concrete track signposted as a bridleway to Geddington, you reach the isolated church seen from afar earlier. It is now a Field Study Centre run by the Newton-in-the-Willows Trust.

The route back to Geddington is straightforward. The bridleway continues past Newton church as a field path. This runs across fields and through gates heading directly for the buildings of Mill Farm, seen clearly ahead. There you meet the road, where you turn right. You can now walk back through Geddington, across the main road and on to the Star Inn.

Places of interest nearby

Boughton Park, the estate surrounding Boughton House, the Duke of Buccleuch's home just south of Geddington, is administered by the Living Landscape Trust. Nature trails, riverside walks and a woodland adventure play area have been laid out for visitors. At Brigstock, 4 miles to the north-east, the *Hill Farm Herbs Centre* is housed in and around a traditional farmhouse.

17 Cranford
The Red Lion

This pub once stood on the main road from Kettering to Thrapston, but has now been by-passed by the A14 trunk road. Nevertheless, it has managed to retain its popularity. This is because it boasts a cosy, friendly atmosphere and serves an excellent range of food and drink. It also has the advantage of being open all day (11 am – 11 pm) every day except Sundays (when more usual pub opening times are kept). Children are well catered for, there being a large slide in the garden.

Inside this fine 18th century building, there are two main rooms, both large and spacious. To one side is the public bar with a television and games facilities; to the other side is a lounge, adjoined to which is a separate eating area. Families use the latter. There are stone walls (decorated with plates and prints), carpets and comfortable 'settle'-type seats. An open fire burns in winter.

The Red Lion serves real ales including Tetleys and Flowers. Apart from the food items on the menu – including hot meat rolls, ploughman's lunches, curries, salads, burgers, scampi and Cumberland sausages – there are daily specials written up on boards. These might include mixed grills or seafood platters. Vegetarians are catered for, as are those with special dietary needs. There are set lunch

menus for both senior citizens and executives. For dessert why not try the luxury ice-cream creations?
Telephone: 01536 330663.

How to get there: Standing midway between Kettering and Thrapston (each is 4 miles away), Cranford will be found immediately north of the A14. It is most easily reached from Barton Seagrave, or from the A14 turn-off to Finedon, which is just one mile to the east. The Red Lion stands on the old through road in that part of Cranford called St John.

Parking: The Red Lion has its own large car park. Cars can also be left along the village roadsides.

Length of the walk: 1½ miles. OS Landranger map 141 Kettering and Corby (inn GR 925768).

This is a lovely little stroll around the twin villages of Cranford St John and Cranford St Andrew. There are no stiles, no steep slopes and no problems with undergrowth. All the paths are firm and dry, being gravel or tarmac. The circuit is especially suitable for those with prams or wheelchairs. There are many old and interesting buildings to look at, and many pleasant views.

The Walk
The stroll begins down the lane opposite the Red Lion. This is called Church Lane and leads down below the trees to a row of thatched cottages. Over to the left of these you will see the post office, an interesting old building with a gable end showing the bricked-up holes to a former pigeon loft. An ancient tavern called The Stag once stood hereabouts.

Bearing right, continuing along Church Lane, you walk alongside the estate boundary wall of Cranford Hall. If you are tall enough, a pleasant view can be had over this wall to the gardens and Hall itself. At the far end is St John's church, dating back to the 12th century. With time permitting, do have a look inside, where there is some fine 16th century Flemish carving and stained glass windows dating from the 15th century.

You now turn left, down the lane called Duck End running northwards from the side of the church. This takes you out of the village. Over to the right, as you walk along this lane, you will see various lumps and bumps in the grassy fields. These are the remnants of old industrial workings.

Soon after passing Duck End Farm, an attractive 18th century building on the right, you come to a lane on the left. This is opposite

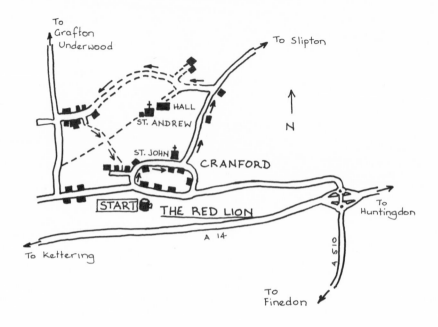

a fine thatched house called Stanbridge Cottage and is marked as a
'Private Road', going to Cranford Hall, The Little House, and Home
Farm. It is indeed private, since you are now entering Cranford Hall
estate and there is – technically – no public right of way through the
grounds. However, quiet sensible walkers are allowed and all the
locals have permitted rights of passage. Visitors are asked if they
would kindly respect the privacy of those who live on the estate.

Continue up the lane, bearing right where you see the entrance
gates to Cranford Hall on the left, and bearing left where you see the
entrance to the farm on the right. In effect, you bend with the lane as
it runs up into open country. The next few hundred yards are
enchanting. Over the hedge on the left are the grounds sweeping up
to the front of Cranford Hall, an elegant Georgian mansion; over the
hedge on the right are the fields stretching into the distance. The
tower of St Andrew's church peeps out from amongst the trees.

Soon you arrive at a gate through which the gravel lane leads into
Cranford St Andrew village, with Dairy Farm back to your left. This
farmhouse is 17th century and was once the manor house to the
village. The lane ahead leads eventually to the Grafton Underwood
road. The Woolpack Inn is along here on the right.

After wandering around a little, or perhaps after some refreshment
at the inn, the journey back to Cranford St John is by way of a public

Cranford Hall.

footpath. This begins opposite the Woolpack (close to a Victorian letter box set into a wall) and runs diagonally across a field usually grazed by sheep. It is surfaced with tarmac. On your way be sure to admire the old dovecote and St Andrew's Church, both over to your left. In the far corner an elegant bridge, constructed of iron and dated 1897, takes you across a little stream and onto the road. The post office is now to your left and the Red Lion is on the far side of the green.

Places of interest nearby

Nearby Kettering has many places to visit, from *Wickstead Park* with its leisure facilities and amusements, to the *Manor House Museum* and *Alfred East Art Gallery*. On the northern outskirts of Kettering, and just 3 miles north-west of Cranford, is *Boughton House*. This splendid building – known as the 'English Versailles' – is owned by the Duke of Buccleuch. Disabled visitors are especially welcome and are well catered for.

⁜ Islip
The Woolpack Hotel

It is said there is a secret tunnel beneath this handsome 16th century building. If so, it could well be connected with medieval Montagu Manor, that once stood in the village high street. This was owned by the Bishops of Coutance, and some of its old stones have since been incorporated into the old cottages near the church. Alternatively the tunnel might be linked to the old wharfs, now gone, that used to line the river Nene. Islip once had important river-bound trade.

The Woolpack today provides a range of services. It offers excellent accommodation facilities, caters for parties and functions and even provides conference rooms. At the rear are pleasant gardens and an attractive Victorian-style conservatory; at the side are the Cream Fleece Tearooms, which are open during the summer months. Yet, with all these features, the whole place has a friendly, homely feel about it.

The Woolpack is a freehouse, offering Boddingtons and Charles Wells' IPA real ales. Since it specialises in food, it provides a full range of both bar snacks and main meals. There are ploughman's lunches, sandwiches, pies, quiches, curries, salads, pasta dishes and so on. Vegetarians are not forgotten. Normal pub opening times are kept.

Telephone: 01832 732578.

How to get there: Islip stands across the river Nene from Thrapston. It is 7 miles east of Kettering and 10 miles north-east of Wellingborough. It lies just north of the A14 trunk road and close to the A6116 road to Corby. The Woolpack Hotel, at the southern end of the village, is very close to the Nene bridge at the edge of Thrapston.

Parking: There is a car park at the front. Vehicles can also be left in the village, provided no obstruction is caused to local drivers.

Length of the walk: 2½ miles. OS Landranger map 141 Kettering and Corby (inn GR 989786).

The whole area north of Islip and Thrapston, as far as Aldwincle and Thorpe Waterville, is a birdwatchers' paradise. On either side of the river Nene, and across the meadows, old gravel workings have been turned into lakes. Nature reserves have been set up and bird habitats encouraged. Woodlands have been planted and wild flowers protected. This short walk gives just a taste of this scenery, at its southern end. But there are many paths and numerous walks that could be enjoyed.

The Walk
From outside The Woolpack Hotel walk eastwards along the main road into Thrapston, crossing the bridge over the river Nene. This river has two different pronunciations locally. Downstream from here – that is, towards Cambridge and the Wash – it is known as the 'Neen'; upstream towards the Northamptonshire Heights it is the 'Nen'.

On your left you pass the Bridge Hotel, Thrapston fire station and the library, eventually turning left up Chancery Lane to the Castle playing fields. This large area of grass is so called because remnants of a mound still survive, once the site of a medieval castle. Those wishing to see Thrapston's fine 13th century church, should take one of the alleyways east of Chancery Lane.

The route continues left, around the top end of the playing fields, along Green Lane, where a footpath signpost will be found opposite the health centre. The track is wide and gravel made. It kinks a little but leads directly to a footbridge over the southern end of Thrapston lake (the largest of the flooded gravel pits), and thence to another footbridge over the river Nene. On the far side of this is Islip Mill. You may wish to cross the river for a closer look – it is an imposing edifice – but the circular walk actually continues to the right before crossing the footbridge.

The path that leads northwards, along the east bank of the river, provides an easy and enjoyable walk. It is a wide gravel track, firm and

85

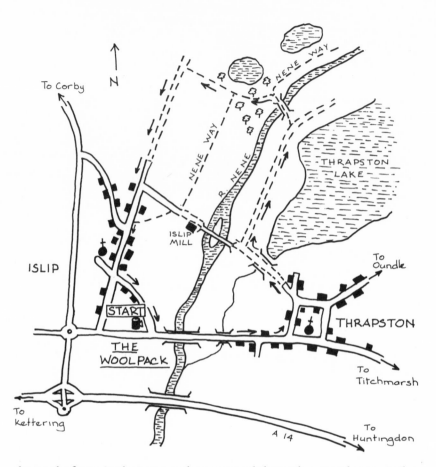

dry underfoot. And once you have passed through a metal gate, at the far end of the sailing club fence which has accompanied you to the right, the views open out.

About half a mile further on, the track, you will notice, comes closer to the lake's shore. Opposite here, some 20 yards over to your left, you will see a footbridge, crossing the Nene. Be careful not to miss it for this is the direction you require.

On the far side of the bridge are two stiles, two arrow discs, and a choice of two paths. Both paths in fact are part of the Nene Way. Take the one going left, which takes you into the woods. The other would lead you northwards to Aldwincle. Before moving on, however, be sure to read the Northamptonshire Wildlife Trust information board.

This section of Nene Way, through the woods, is the prettiest part of the circular walk. The route is clear, the undergrowth is speckled

Islip church.

with wild flowers and the spreading branches above give a dappled shade. To the right are glimpses of a lake, a much smaller one than that seen earlier. Many little woods and copses have been planted across these meadows, mostly with alders and willows.

When you reach the edge of this particular area of trees a signpost points the way left, across a field. This is the Nene Way, heading back to Islip Mill. You could follow that route but our circular walk actually continues straight on, keeping to the southern edge of the woodland. In due course you emerge onto a wide gravel track. There are open fields ahead and a gate to your left. Go through the gate and follow the track southwards. It will take you straight to Islip village.

This last half mile is pleasant. The track – which is actually labelled as a bridleway – is called Ridge Road. It is well named, for it offers views in both directions; left across the Nene and its watery meadows, right towards Drayton Park. Ahead is the spire of Islip church.

Once back in the village you continue straight on along the main street. St Nicholas' church, on the right, is a fine example of Perpendicular Gothic architecture.

Other buildings are also worth noticing, not least the old cottages mentioned earlier that are thought to contain stonework from the original Montagu Manor. But, in the absence of any secret tunnel, the best way back to the Woolpack from here is down the High Street, turning left at the fork.

Places of interest nearby
Those interested in the lakes and nature reserves north of Thrapston will also enjoy *Lilford Park* (4 miles north-east of Islip). *Lyveden New Bield*, 4 miles north of Islip, is one of the many constructions erected by Sir Thomas Tresham in the 17th century. Now owned by the National Trust it is little more than a shell, since it was never finished. The village of Barnwell (south of Oundle) should also be visited, with its old cottages, derelict church, country park (with disabled facilities) and manor house whose gardens can be viewed on certain days each year.

Bulwick
19 The Queens Head Inn

Dating from the second half of the 17th century, this building was once three cottages. These must have been very small, for the Queens Head is not exactly a large pub now, and some additions have been made since its early days. Entrance is gained at the rear, from the car park, and the interior is divided into two parts. To the right is a small, quiet, dining area, doubling as a lounge used by families. To the left is the larger bar room, used by locals and others who prefer a more convivial atmosphere. All around there are areas of bare stone walls (including two chimney breasts), woodwork (including beams hung with horsebrasses and tankards) and traditional pub decor (with pictures and plates fixed to the walls). In winter months open fires burn, making the surroundings even more cosy.

As a freehouse the Queens Head serves real ales like Bateman and Abbot Ale, and various wines. There is an extensive menu, this being supplemented with a daily specials board on the bar room wall. The choice of food is consequently wide, ranging from bar snacks like sandwiches, ploughman's lunches and burgers to full meals like meat pies, steaks, chops, and fish dishes. Vegetarians are offered vegetable and pasta bakes.

Normal pub opening times are kept. The Queens Head is a friendly, welcoming place where families are made to feel at home.
Telephone: 01780 450272.

How to get there: Bulwick, in the north-east of the county, will be found just 6 miles from Corby and 12 miles from Kettering. It stands close to the A43 road, which links those towns with Stamford and the A1 trunk road. The Queens Head is situated in the middle of the village, opposite the church.

Parking: There is a large car park behind the pub. Vehicles can also be left along the roadsides of Bulwick. Since the village has been by-passed the place has become pleasantly quiet so parking is not a problem.

Length of the walk: 5 miles (or shorter options). OS Landranger map 141 Kettering and Corby (inn GR 963943).

This walk is to Deene and back. Deene is a pretty village situated at the edge of the landscaped estate of Deene Park, and dominated by Deene Hall, one-time home of the Brudenell family. The route there lies along the banks of the Willow Brook, whose valley is remarkably unspoilt. The route back from Deene is by way of country lanes and bridleways. Those wishing to shorten the circuit can do so, for many return options present themselves. The scenery throughout this walk is pleasantly rural with broad horizons across farmlands and willow-scattered meadows. The route is clear throughout and the ground generally firm underfoot.

The Walk
The path to Deene begins next to the Queens Head. It runs up beside the car park, past a cottage on the right and through a stile beyond. The first field you cross is very interesting. As part of the Bulwick Hall estate it has been landscaped into a 'parkland' with scattered trees, but the undulations hide a medieval landscape: the original village once stood here.

The route is not difficult to follow. Keeping the river parallel, and down a little way to your right, continue across the field to a stile a short distance to the left of the far corner. Follow the edge of the next field before bearing right, shortly before the end, to dip down through the trees to another stile. The main A43 road, which by-passes Bulwick, is up on the embankment beyond. Cross this road carefully, and continue along the footpath on the other side. In fact, you must go right and left across the road (over the Willow Brook) because the next stretch of footpath runs along the other bank.

Below the road embankment a stile and signpost will be found. The

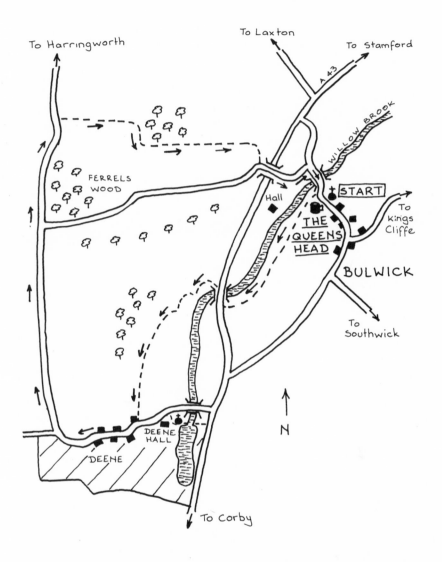

To Laxton

To Harringworth

To Stamford

A 43

WILLOW BROOK

FERRELS WOOD

Hall

START

THE QUEENS HEAD

To Kings Cliffe

BULWICK

To Southwick

N

DEENE HALL

DEENE

To Corby

path now bears left a little to meander through the willows and meadow vegetation of Willow Brook valley. Some footbridges along here carry you over some ditches. At the edge of the trees a stile over a wire fence leads to a large field. Continue across this in the same direction as before, keeping the woodland on the skyline to your half-right. A further stile, another field and a further stile are all encountered, as you keep in the same direction. Soon the houses of

91

Deene village are visible ahead. Across the last field, as you aim for the village hall – a stone building – be sure to admire the view to the left, of Deene Hall and, further away, Deene church. A gate in the corner brings you to the village street.

Those wishing to return to Bulwick the short way, and see more of Deene Park, should turn left, and proceed down the road to the church from where a footpath leads across the parkland by the lake. A return can thence be made along the old A43. All others should turn right and walk all the way through the village. Deene is a handsome, stone-built village, constructed mainly in the 18th century to replace the old settlement which now stands below the lake in the Park. On your way through Deene you can admire the thatched houses and, on the right, part of the old manor house, now Manor Farm.

Beyond the village keep right at the junction to follow the direction to Harringworth and Seaton. A 1½ mile road walk now follows, but this is not unpleasant. Those wishing to curtail the circular walk can turn right at the road junction before Ferrels Wood and walk down the lane signposted to Bulwick. Others should continue to a point beyond Ferrels Wood where a public bridleway sign points right, across a large field.

This last stretch is very clear. The bridleway consists of a wide, double-rutted track, gravelly in parts. This runs almost dead straight for half a mile, until it reaches a patch of woodland called Bantrup Bushes. It then turns right to keep the woodland on its left-hand side, and then (just beyond the trees) left to run along a valley keeping the stream some little distance to the right-hand side. At the far end a right bend brings you to a lane that crosses over the A43 by-pass road. Bulwick is now immediately ahead and can be reached by keeping to the lane turning left, then right, as you go.

This last bridleway section should not be rushed, for the countryside is very unspoilt here. Early on, Luxton church spire can be seen on the left horizon, later Bulwick church spire can be seen ahead.

Places of interest nearby

There are several stately homes to visit nearby. *Deene House*, and its surrounding estate, is open on summer Sundays. Further west, by just a mile, is the splendid ruin of *Kirby Hall*. This Elizabethan mansion is now just a shell, but the architecture remains awe-inspiring. The gardens are being restored. *Southwick Hall* (4 miles east of Bulwick) dates from the 14th century and is open three days a week in summer. Just a couple of miles north of Bulwick are *Wakerley Great Wood* and *Fineshade Wood*, Forestry Commission lands that now offer facilities for visitors. Both have nature trails.

20 Nassington
The Black Horse Inn

This 'listed' building is of great architectural and historic interest. Not only does it date from the 17th century, but it also contains a bar front made up of old doors from Rufford Abbey and a fireplace from nearby Fotheringhay Castle. The latter was discovered in 1976 during restoration work. It was evidently brought here soon after the castle itself fell into disrepair, in the years following the execution there in 1587 of Mary Queen of Scots.

The Black Horse today specialises in food, and its menus have won various awards. To the left of the bar room as you enter is the Garden Room, laid out as a restaurant; to the right is another large dining area. No list here could do justice to the food selection provided, and no-one should be disappointed. Bar snacks include seafood pancakes, soups, pâtés, cheese fritters and steak sandwiches, main meals include escalopes, scampi, various poultry dishes and pasta bakes. There are vegetarian and children's menus, and all manner of tempting desserts. Apart from the standard items, daily specials are listed on the blackboards. This freehouse is open normal pub times. The real ales served include Bass and Tetley and there is an extensive wine list.

Telephone: 01780 782324.

How to get there: Nassington is very close to the Cambridgeshire border, and is only 8 miles from the centre of Peterborough. Stamford, in the southern corner of Lincolnshire, is 6 miles northwards, Oundle is 5 miles southwards. The Black Horse stands at the south-east corner of the village, at the corner of the Fotheringhay road.

Parking: There is a pub car park.

Length of the walk: 3 miles. OS Landranger map 142 Peterborough (inn GR 067962).

This walk is to Yarwell and back. The outward route follows part of the Nene Way, the long distance footpath that runs the length of Northamptonshire from Badby to Wansford. The return journey follows an old byway. The route is well marked and well used. The meadows of the river Nene are especially attractive at this end of the county, notwithstanding their closeness to Peterborough.

The Walk

The Nene Way will be found very close to the Black Horse – less than 100 yards away on the other side of the road. To reach it, turn right outside the pub and walk away from the village. You will see the gate, stile and arrow disc on the left-hand side.

The route is clearly marked all the way, with regular arrow discs. A clear track leads down the edge of a field to a bridge across the Nene river and thence along the edge of another field to a stile and gate. Across the following field you aim diagonally to the half left, reaching another stile that leads you over a narrow water channel. Just 20 yards beyond this a choice presents itself. To follow the circuit as planned turn right here, across a stile, and stride over the river Nene using concrete blocks which are set into the water as stepping stones. To shorten the circuit and in so doing, miss out this invigorating traverse, continue straight on along the edge of the field keeping the hedgerow and river to your right.

Having to cross the Nene twice may seem odd, but the river, in fact, divides along this stretch. There are two wide water channels here. The first you crossed was that length used by pleasure craft, the second was the fast-flowing uncanalised river section.

From the stepping stones turn left and follow the river bank northwards. The path runs along a field edge, through a patch of bushes and trees, across a stile and back over the river by way of an old bridge which once carried a railway line. From there you follow the edge of a woodland, which is to your right, and then through a thicket to a kissing gate. Beyond this, cross the bridge and sluice-gate to Yarwell Mill. Here is the canal arm of the Nene and pleasure craft

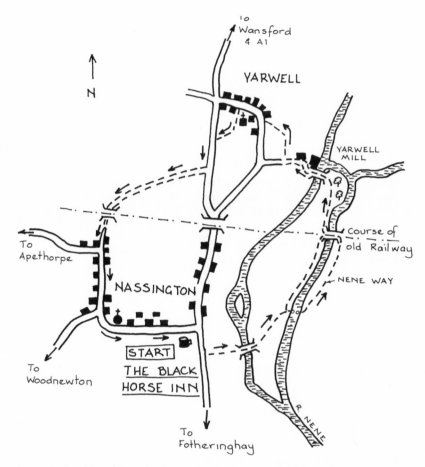

abound. Incidentally, during your walk from the stepping stones to this mill you have been, briefly, in Cambridgeshire.

Yarwell Mill is a busy little place, with a camping site. To leave it behind turn left after walking across the front of the mill and then, after passing a farm on your right, turn right along a footpath that starts from a stile set high on the grassy bank. This continuation of the Nene Way leads through two fields and takes you directly to Yarwell village.

When you reach the road turn right to walk through the main part of the village, where stands an interesting 13th century church and the very inviting Angel Inn. During the 18th and 19th centuries Yarwell was an important stone-working village, with numerous quarries dotted around and many masons living here.

Fotheringhay church.

The route back to Nassington begins either along the main village street, turning left at the junction, or along the footpath that runs up to the left after passing the church. The latter is signposted as a footpath to Nassington. It runs up by a field edge, over a stile and then right alongside the playing field to the road. Here you turn left.

Less than half a mile along this road, south of Yarwell, a wide gravel track leads off to the right, to run between hedgerows. A signpost calls it a 'Byway', and local maps call it Ruisbrick Lane. In due course it becomes an earth and grass track – but very clear and very pleasant. It passes under the old railway line and ends at the northern edge of Nassington. There you continue straight on past the housing estates and left at the church. The Black Horse is at the bottom of the hill.

Places of interest nearby

The Nassington *Prebendal Manor House*, opposite the church, dates from the early 13th century. It is open on three afternoons per week in summer months. At *Fotheringhay*, 2 miles south of Nassington, is another ecclesiastical site. The church there dominates the skyline. Nearby is the mound that was once the castle where Mary Queen of Scots was executed.